Stay Ready

2025 EDITION

Beau Cisco, M.S.

BEHAVIORAL ANALYSIS TRAINING GROUP

ISBN: 9798649332231

Dedication

This work is dedicated to my family for their love and support through the long hours and time away from home in order to make this happen.

More especially to the two little voices that would say

"Go teach your friends, Dada"

Acknowledgments

I would like to acknowledge the following people for making this work possible:

The men and women of the Palm Beach County Sheriff's Office for their professionalism and friendship.

The Austin Police Department Field Training Officer's circa 1999 in "Charlie Sector" whom I believed had failed me at the time but became my biggest motivators to succeed.

To Christopher Olivero for his persistence back in 2007 which convinced me to start teaching.

CONTENTS

INTRODUCTION

I was two hours into my shift when I stopped by a local coffee shop with my partner for a much-needed cup of coffee. It was 7:00 a.m., and the shop had about fifteen patrons, each starting their day. My partner and I were patrol sergeants, each with about twenty years on the job, working in one of the highest-crime areas in our agency's jurisdiction. As we sat discussing a case, our attention was drawn to the front door, where two fellow officers entered. They were both new to law enforcement and had recently started their first day on our shift.

As I watched, I noticed them scanning the room before flinching slightly upon spotting their supervisors sitting in the corner. I imagined them mentally wrestling with whether it was "okay to be here" before proceeding to the counter to order. Once they had their coffee, we motioned for them to join us.

Out of curiosity, I singled out one of the officers and asked, "What were you scanning for when you walked through the front door?"

His response was quick and confident: "Threats."

I did my best to look intrigued as I asked, "What do threats look like?"

His answer was similar to the many I've received over the years—he was looking for a crime in progress, "suspicious activity," or perhaps a man in the corner slapping a magazine into an AK-47. I smiled and took a sip of my coffee.

"Did you happen to notice the two men sitting across from us who haven't stopped watching us since we walked in? Or the fact that they glance at the door every time one of us looks in that direction? What about the woman sitting by the door who clutched her purse and pulled it closer when you walked by—and now appears nervous?"

My partner and I smiled as we took in the blank stares sitting across from us.

The new officer wasn't wrong—his examples showed risk. However, there is a significant failure in law enforcement training when it comes to situational awareness. In my two decades in law enforcement and through countless training classes, I can't say I've been taught much about situational awareness beyond simply being told to "be aware" of my surroundings. As a profession, we sell ourselves short by not incorporating the vast knowledge of body language and psychology available to us.

If I had only prompted the new officer to look for certain behaviors, he would have been more aware of the other coffee shop patrons. In his mind, he was focused solely on threats, and that's all he was looking for. He didn't have a plan because he didn't know what to look for or how to find it. His academy instructors had drilled into him the importance of being aware, yet they provided few actual tools to achieve it. If you only look for threats, that's all you'll see— and therein lies the pitfall.

This training will focus on learning to read body language. We're not looking for threats. In fact, we're not looking for anything specific. We are simply listening and observing what is being communicated to us by everyone around us.

Another goal of this book is to give you the vocabulary to describe what you see. Often, we observe behavior but struggle to articulate it in words. The ability to explain what you see is paramount in understanding human behavior. Not only does it help you interpret the world around you, but it also allows you to articulate your observations and justify your actions when necessary. Additionally, being able to articulate observations helps you form a plan based on those observations. As we will explore later, having a plan for what you observe is one of the most important aspects of situational awareness training.

Understanding those around you through body language is not a difficult task, but it does require dedication and time. First, you must understand how thought processes work in conjunction with the body. While that may sound complicated, it's actually quite simple. We all know the brain is the source of emotions, decisions, fears, aspirations, and mindset. The rest of the body responds instantly, obeying even the slightest impulse or fleeting thought.

To illustrate this, imagine the following scenario:

It's early Monday morning, and you're walking down the hallway at work. As you approach a coworker from the opposite direction, you nod and say, "Good morning, how are you?" To your regret, they stop and begin to recount, in great detail, the highs and lows of their life. You quickly realize your mistake and immediately wish you hadn't initiated the conversation. You're now trapped in a hallway monologue, held hostage by someone who may never stop talking.

At first, you try to be polite, waiting for a break in the conversation so you can excuse yourself. The problem? That break never comes. You're stuck listening to endless stories, complaints, and questions that don't interest you in the slightest.

At this moment, just like in the TV shows we grew up with, a little angel appears on your right shoulder, and a small devil appears on your left.

The angel whispers, "Be patient. This person is troubled. Listen a little longer, then excuse yourself politely."

The devil, on the other hand, loudly suggests, "Walk away. Tell them to shut up. Maybe even scream obscenities in their direction for this unprovoked kidnapping."

As the angel and devil argue, your brain becomes locked in an internal debate—stay or go? Meanwhile, your body listens intently and attempts to follow orders. But all it hears is "Go… Stay… Go… Stay."

Your body, ever obedient to the brain's slightest whim, reacts accordingly. At the first hint of "GO," your right foot shifts slightly in the direction you originally intended to go—but then it stops when it hears "STAY." At the start of this conversation, your feet were fully facing the talkative coworker. Now, one foot is pointed slightly down the hallway. As time passes and your brain continues this internal tug-of-war, your stance shifts subtly, your body leaning more and more in the direction of your intended path.

This is the essence of body language. Even though you didn't consciously tell your body to leave, your thoughts influenced your movement. The emotions, fears, and decisions your brain processes are reflected in your physical actions, often without you realizing it.

At this point in the book, this concept may seem abstract. However, as you continue reading, you'll see in detail how your mindset controls your movement and how others reveal their thoughts through their own body language.

Now that we've started to explore how the brain and body interact, it should be clear that much of your performance and awareness is directly linked to your mindset. In the following chapters, we will cover a variety of body language examples to help you better understand the people around you. While the study of body language is vast, we have distilled the most critical aspects to make them easy to understand and applicable to your daily life.

When the rookie officer attempted to scan the coffee shop, he didn't have a plan, so his scan was basic at best. His goal was to look for threats, but with limited experience, he focused only on overt dangers—no one was loading an AK-47 magazine or actively committing a crime, so everything else went unnoticed.

As you progress through this book, you will begin to understand what people are "saying" around you. One of the most important principles of this book is having a plan. I will periodically outline key behaviors to watch for, but it is ultimately your responsibility to develop a plan for observation. When you walk into a coffee shop, don't just glance around—think about what you are going to look for.

Situational awareness is not about expecting threats. It's about understanding behavior.

CHAPTER 1

Complacency

Understanding the silent killer

The Merriam-Webster Dictionary defines **complacency** as: *"marked by self-satisfaction, especially when accompanied by unawareness of actual dangers or deficiencies."*

I spoke to a traffic officer with over 20 years of experience and asked him how many traffic stops he had performed throughout his career. His response? Around 10,000. I marveled at the number and then asked how many shootings, fights, or critical incidents he had been involved in. His response? Only a handful. I wondered to myself: *If I did the same thing 10,000 times, could I still remain mentally alert and focused every single time?*

I think we have all heard warnings throughout our training and careers to avoid complacency at all costs. I do not fault this logic in any way, but it does not take into account that we are all human. While being complacent in a high-risk profession such as law enforcement or corrections carries significant risks, we still need to examine it practically.

I consider myself an alert professional who puts an extraordinary amount of effort into doing my job well. Yet, I have come to work on two hours of sleep because of young children. I have spent entire shifts distracted by an argument with my wife. I have felt frustration and burnout when I saw less deserving colleagues get promoted ahead of me. I have been exhausted and simply *not wanted to be there*. These are all human experiences, and nearly everyone goes through them at some point. We do our best to push forward, even when life wears us down.

I feel complacency is widely misunderstood in our profession. We are constantly reminded *never* to be complacent, yet complacency is part of a natural cycle of human behavior. We simply cannot expect to be completely focused for every second of our careers. How does complacency not become part of my behavior profile, at least occasionally? We all know it only takes *one time* for a critical mistake to happen, so is it just luck that we're still here?

I want you to understand that complacency is a natural part of this job and that you will be complacent more times than you will care to admit to anyone. However, this does not mean you are doomed to become one of those training videos showing an officer getting seriously injured because they failed to notice the warning signs of another's behavior.

The average officer's understanding of complacency stems from the belief that they "were just not paying attention" or that they "became careless in their actions." This often manifests in ways such as disregarding basic safety principles, conducting lazy or ineffective searches, poor vehicle placement on calls, unsafe distances when interacting with potential adversaries, and other behaviors that can be seen as "cutting corners."

Training must account for complacency. You must train in a manner that fosters an understanding of behaviors and forces you, through repetition, to be observant—so that even on the days when your mind is elsewhere, you still remain aware of your surroundings and become alert when necessary.

I cannot imagine myself at peak alertness every day of my career for 30 years. However, I do expect myself to train in a way that allows me, even on days when I am not at my best, to recognize what is happening around me, assess potential dangers, and act accordingly and with purpose.

Cognitive biases are part of human psychology, and it is important not to view them solely as negatives. We must **accept** that they are part of our psyche and learn to work *with* them, rather than ignore or suppress them. While this section of the book will discuss biases in terms of the risks they pose, these psychological mechanisms are fundamental to how we think, act, and perceive the world. They are shaped by our experiences, training, education, and personal comfort levels in various situations. By understanding that biases exist and recognizing their effects, you will gain a better understanding of how to incorporate them into your decision-making process.

Now, let's examine a psychological aspect of complacency.

On June 14, 2019, Republican members of the U.S. Congress were playing in a charity baseball game in Alexandria, Virginia. A man armed with an assault rifle entered the stadium and began shooting at congressional representatives and bystanders. A reporter and photographer named Marty LaVor, who was covering the event, later said:

"He picked up the rifle, and so I saw the rifle, and the thought that ran through my mind ... because it was so out of context, why would anybody have a rifle there? And what ran through my mind was, 'Why would anybody be trying to shoot birds at six o'clock in the morning?'" (Chappell, 2017)

While this may not seem logical, it is a textbook example of **normalcy bias**—our tendency to interpret unusual events in a way that makes them seem normal.

It is highly unusual to see a man walk into a baseball stadium with a rifle. Many in law enforcement would immediately assume he was there to harm people. However, civilians, who are not conditioned to expect violence, often rationalize the situation in a way that fits their existing worldview. In this case, the photographer unconsciously altered reality to make sense of it—he assumed the man was there to shoot birds.

Now, consider the traffic officer who conducted 10,000 traffic stops with virtually no critical incidents over 20 years. While he understands there is always *some* risk, his normalcy bias may lead him to believe that *this* traffic stop is just like all the others. If he unconsciously dismisses subtle red flags, that could put him in danger.

On June 25, 2009, Sergeant Mark Chesnut made a traffic stop outside Nashville, Tennessee, for a seatbelt violation. Upon addressing the occupants, the dashcam video later revealed numerous inconsistencies in their stories—discrepancies about where the car was rented, their destination, the purpose of their trip, and where they had come from. Sgt. Chesnut even noticed a pair of handcuffs in the backseat. Despite these warning signs, he returned to his vehicle to make a phone call, leaving one of the occupants unattended.

The amount of suspicious behavior, deception cues, and pre-violence indicators in this case was staggering. Yet minutes later, Sgt. Chesnut was shot six times and nearly lost his life.

I do not share this story to cast dishonor on Sgt. Chesnut or his unfortunate circumstances. Instead, I present it so we can ask ourselves: *Why do these incidents happen?* More importantly, *how can we train future officers to prevent similar situations?*

In an interview published on PoliceOne.com, Sgt. Chesnut reflected on the shooting and admitted that, when he saw the handcuffs, he assumed:

"These guys must be a couple of rogue bounty hunters as well as drug mules." (Remsberg, 2011)

He likely believed this because of past experiences with similar situations. Since he had encountered "rogue bounty hunters running dope" before without issue, his normalcy bias led him to feel safe and in control—even though the warning signs were there.

This case also illustrates **investigative blindness**—the tendency for officers to focus so heavily on one assumption about a case that they fail to consider other possibilities. When everything *feels* normal and comfortable, why would we look deeper?

Understanding the psychological and behavioral factors that influence complacency is the first step in overcoming it. Training should not simply tell officers to "never be complacent." Instead, it should acknowledge the reality of human limitations and teach strategies to mitigate them.

By building habits of awareness through repetition and conditioning, we can train ourselves to stay engaged—even on days when we are tired, distracted, or burned out. Through this approach, we can significantly reduce the risks associated with complacency and ensure we remain safe and effective throughout our careers.

Sergeant Mark Chesnut, Nashville Police Department, 2005

On December 14, 2009, PoliceOne.com published an interview titled "Shot 5 times. A sergeant reflects on lessons learned," that mentioned many of the indicators that I just listed, but when he saw the handcuffs, "I thought these guys must be a couple of rogue bounty hunters as well as drug mules," (Remsberg, 2011) He may have believed this was the case due to past experiences with similar circumstances. He felt safe because he had survived those encounters with little or no negative events. Therefore, this case seemed normal, and he felt in control, despite evidence to the contrary. Sergeant Chesnut felt the actions and behaviors of these individuals were consistent with "rogue bounty hunters running dope" and did not look further. The situation felt normal and therefore, he felt comfortable and in control. I'm not making Excuses for Sgt. Chesnut or other officers that have acted in similar manners. I am however, showing you that there are reasons for behaviors, and they are completely avoidable with a positive mindset and a little training.

This event also is an excellent example of what I like to call investigative blindness, which is the unfortunate mindset of officers to think that once they have identified the type of case/crime they are working, it is difficult for them to conceive that there are other things happening also. After all, when everything seems normal and comfortable, why would you look further?

Change Blindness

Another psychological factor that plays a role in our situational awareness is called "change blindness." "Change blindness is the finding that observers often fail to notice large changes to objects or scenes when the change coincides with a brief visual disruption." (Daniel J. Simpson, 2003) says change blindness is a highly studied aspect of human psychology where the brain focuses more on the overall situation rather than the small events. Several university studies have conducted experiments, or a man asks somebody for directions on the street, as they are receiving directions confederates in the experiment work by carrying a large signboard or mirror and therefore, temporarily separating the person asking and the person giving directions. During this time, one of the people carrying the board will still fully replace themselves with the person asking for directions. In some cases, 40 to 60% of the time, the switch goes unnoticed. In several cases, they have switched sexes, races, clothing, and other physical attributes that also went unnoticed. The reasoning for such a phenomenon is largely a factor of attention. This occurs when an individual becomes so focused on an event or situation that they do not notice the small details. A famous experiment dealing with change blindness involved a video where several students dressed in black shirts and several students dressed in white shirts were passing a basketball to each other in a group. Participants in this experiment were asked to count the number of passes by those wearing a white shirt and while a substantial number reported the correct number of passes, they did not see a man in a gorilla suit walk through the crowd of people. (Christopher Chabris, 2010)

While we are likely to see a man and a gorilla walk through one of our calls and or scenes, we often miss or overlook minute details such as body language, deception cues, and pre-attack indicators on a regular basis. While they may seem very unrelated, I assure you that that is not the case. We tend to miss small facts and details because we are focused on the big picture. In many cases, this is because of high stress, exhaustion, confusion, or overconfidence.

In the pursuit of striving to avoid complacency in our daily work environment, we must also understand the physical and psychological limitations our brain has. Understanding these things is the first step in this training and by continuing this book, you will learn over time to overcome these limitations and greatly diminish your chances of complacency.

Training and Operations

When we think about complacency in the context of behavioral awareness, we must consider our training and socialization. Most people feel they have an acceptable level of situational awareness yet in many casual conversations most people cannot answer simple questions about what's going on around them. While I am not interested in the common situational awareness belief that you should be memorizing how many chairs are in a room or license plate in a parking lot, those are for the TV spy. I am interested in enabling you to become more aware of the behaviors around you. Throughout this book, I will stress that training and socialization philosophy must be adopted to be able to use the items in this book. Chiefly, we are looking to erase the behaviors that build with complacency and replace them with more effective habits and understanding your behavior.

When people fear they are in danger their situational and behavioral awareness peaks due to a survival instinct that we all have. The problem is, countless times you will read about victims repeatedly saying, "I never saw it coming" or "I was not expecting it, it came out of nowhere" and other statements similar to these. One of the biggest obstacles in developing behavioral awareness is that it needs to be constantly active. I do not feel that people should or even can be in a constant state of alert every waking moment, this is a recipe for disaster and burning out. Yet, it would seem the necessity is real. This is where our training comes into play, or lack thereof. The average officer will engage in thousands of hours of training throughout the course of his career. This will stem from academy, added training classes, service training, professional development courses, online and video training and training each day at the beginning of shift. In this section, we will discuss the aspects of training law enforcement and how we correctly and incorrectly implement that training in the field.

During our agency's yearly training, I was watching three instructors show seasoned officers how to tactically enter a room during a building search. The training was significantly different from the training in previous years for tactically entering rooms. As I sat there watching the class, I was distracted by a group of newer officers sitting next to me. I could hear them grumbling over the fact that the instructors had admonished them for questioning why the training was different this year. One of the officers was sharing his plan to just finish the training and go back to how he's always done it. The other officers nodded in agreeance and had made up their mind that this training was just the training division's way of justifying their existence. I addressed the officers and asked them, "Have you ever thought that they are not replacing existing training, but teaching a new method to show that we have more options in the field?" Sadly, none of the officers had thought that because the instructors had not presented it that way.

When we contemplate that last example, we can take a guess that this training will have extraordinarily little impact on the officers' performance. It is also safe to assume that any positive benefits that were intended with the training are probably lost given the officers' mindset. We will now explore how mindset affects our learning and training in both law enforcement training as well as the behavioral awareness training that will come later in this book.

Colonel David Grossman has authored several books where he discusses the mindset in law enforcement and military training and operations. He speaks about how in stressful situations we will fall back on our training. For the most part this is a true statement and one of the main reasons the military and law enforcement train so stringently with tactics, weapons and fighting because it is the training we hope to fall back on when we are at our most stressed. However, one of the fallacies in this thinking is that we are only likely to fall back on the training that we gave our "heart and soul" to.

I recall a class in the police academy when we were learning defensive tactics. During one of our lessons, the instructors had set up several punching bags, each designed for a different punch or kick. As we rotated through the stations we would punch or kick as we were instructed to for a set time and then move to the next station. The instructor repeated over again for us to "take it seriously" as we punched and kicked the bags. He asked us to imagine a scenario where we were fighting for our lives as we punched and kicked at each station. Despite these instructions, I would look around the room at the other recruits and see that many of them we're not taking this instruction seriously and that they were just going through the motions of punching and kicking the bags with little or no ferocity. *When it comes time to use these skills in a real-life and high stress environment will those who did not apply the proper mindset in training be as successful as those who did?* The short answer is no. The use of proper mindset during training is as important as the technique when you are hoping to have the ability to recall under stress.

This is one of the building blocks of the complacency mindset. Were the recruits were not taking the training seriously because they felt they did not need the extra training, did they feel "it won't happen to me" or did they simply not understand the dangers of the job?

I recall several "after school special" tv show while growing up where a bully had challenged a weaker kid to a fight after school. The weaker kid agonized the entire day on how to avoid the fight. It would make sense the weaker kid never put any effort into fighting or simply never thought he would ever need it.

When we examine complacency, we need to understand how the mind works. In this case, it is important to consider what we take seriously and how we make decisions based on that. We all have a lifetime of lessons learned, teachings, mistakes, successes and failures that guide our decision-making process. We call this experience, and we let it guide the way we navigate through life. Psychology would label this type of experience as cognitive biases. (Tversky, 1974) These are shortcuts in decision making processes based on our "experiences". In some cases, they increase our efficiency by allowing us to make a quick decision without deliberation, which can be a positive outcome from some decisions. On the negative side, cognitive biases can distort our thinking and allow us to "jump to conclusions", make "snap decisions" and fall into lazy thought processes.

I have listed several cognitive biases that will go with nearly every person when engaging in law enforcement work or situational and behavioral awareness. I have given a brief description but also included is a phrase or statement that we have probably all said under certain circumstances. Please pay special attention to the italicized wording and the definitions to understand that we are all affected by bias.

Authority bias	The tendency to place more importance on the opinions of an individual because of their perceived authority or position. *"He's been doing this forever; he must be right"*
Bandwagon effect	The tendency to act or believe in certain ways because many others do also. *"Things like that are just TV nonsense, everybody knows the odds are very small"*
Anchoring bias	The tendency to make decisions heavily is based on only one piece of information. *"I don't see any threats, there won't be any problems today"*

<u>Confirmation bias</u>	The tendency to focus or recall only information that matches a preconception. *"We constantly check for threats and barely see any, let's move on."*
<u>Group attribution bias</u>	The tendency to believe that characteristics or actions of an individual member of a group is attributed to the entire group. "He's not dangerous, I know lots of homeless people and they are harmless"
<u>Dunning–Kruger effect</u>	The tendency for inexperienced individuals to overestimate their abilities (and experts to underestimate their own) *"I've been taught how to do this/I am an expert; I can manage anything"*
<u>Focusing effect</u>	The tendency to overfocus or simply too much importance on only one aspect of an event (Also see Anchoring) *"I don't see anyone who is a problem, we can all relax for now"*
<u>Self-serving bias</u>	The tendency to recall past outcomes and see information only in ways beneficial to themselves. *"It wasn't my fault, no one could have seen that coming"*
<u>Hostile attribution bias</u>	The tendency to see other's behaviors as hostile without just cause. *"When you go into this neighborhood, everyone is out to get you, no matter how they seem"*
<u>Illusion of control</u>	The tendency to overestimate one's level of influence over a series of events. *"You can relax, as long as I am here, there won't be any problems"*

Illusion of validity	The tendency to believe one's choices or actions are correct despite having no corroborating information. *"I read a book about being aware, I know what I am doing"*
Negativity bias	The tendency to recall negative events more often than positive ones. *"No matter what decision we make, they will always say it was wrong"*
Normalcy bias	The tendency to believe in the status quo and refuse to prepare or plan for disaster. *"There is no need to overreact, everything will be fine"*
Optimism bias	The tendency to rely on positive outcomes and overlook the possibility of negative outcomes. *"There is no need to worry about anything, everything will be fine"*
Ostrich effect	The tendency to ignore a negative situation despite overwhelming evidence. *"Just act natural, it will go away"*
Outcome bias	The tendency to judge a situation or event based on the outcome and not the process and decisions made during *"Everything turned out fine, I am sure you did everything right"*
Regressive bias	The tendency to place little value or attention on unlikely events. *"Do you realize how unlikely the odds are for an ambush?"*
Risk compensation bias	The tendency is more daring and forward when you feel safety is not endangered. *"I just finished reading a book on situational awareness. Let's go, I'll see anything out of the ordinary"*

<u>Semmelweis reflex</u>	The tendency to reject ideas or evidence that contradicts a belief. *"Things like that don't really happen, stop bringing it up."*
<u>Subjective validation</u>	The tendency to place a higher degree of fact on coincidences to prove a point. *"This place is very dangerous, there was a robbery here last week"*
<u>Zero-risk bias</u>	The tendency when faced with multiple risks, addressing minor risks instead or more important risks. *"I just bought a gun; I don't have to worry about being a victim anymore"*

Reticular Activating System (RAS)

When we speak of behavioral awareness, complacency, situational awareness, and general mindset, we must consider how the brain works. Few people take the time to investigate the brain's function in relation to the **reticular activating system** (RAS) and its role in situational awareness.

The RAS is a network of neurons found in the brainstem that mediates behavior and mindset. It has a variety of functions, but most notably, it takes what you are focused on and creates a **filter** for it. In short, it sifts through all the data you take in through your senses and decides what you need to be aware of. This determination is based on your

needs, environment, and mindset. While this ability is beneficial, it also causes you to **miss** a great deal of what is happening around you.

For example, imagine you are sitting in the stands at a baseball game. As usual, the crowd is loud and enthusiastic. Most of us are not listening to every conversation, cheer, or sales pitch from a passing hot dog vendor, especially if we are actively watching the game. These background sounds are filtered out by the RAS. You likely miss 99% of the noise around you, yet somehow, you hear your friend several rows back yelling your name. The sound of your name is able to **cut through** the background noise your RAS was actively tuning out because your brain has determined it to be **important**.

In the same way, the RAS also **shapes** your beliefs and mindset based on the parameters you give it. If you believe you are walking through a **safe** neighborhood, and you feel **comfortable** in that environment, you may **overlook** potential danger signals from a person approaching you on the sidewalk. This does not mean you will miss **obvious** threats, such as a man charging at you with a knife, but it does mean that your mind may **relax** to the point that you fail to notice **subtler** warning signs.

While I have greatly simplified the functions of the RAS, it is important to recognize that it **benefits** us as well. Simply walking down a street provides us with **millions** of sensations in the form of sights, sounds, smells, and physical feelings. The RAS considers our mindset and

filters what we need to know. If we were aware of **everything** all at once, we would be mentally overwhelmed in seconds.

- **Example 1**: I have overslept and am now late for an important meeting at work. As I walk down the street to my office building, I am keenly aware that I am in a hurry. My RAS filters out distractions, such as a sale at my favorite store, acquaintances who might stop to talk, and anything else that might slow me down.
- **Example 2**: A traffic officer conducting a routine stop perceives the driver's actions as non-threatening. As a result, he **fails to notice** that the man is carrying a weapon and maneuvering into a position to attack.

The benefit of the RAS is that, while it **filters out** unneeded or unwanted stimuli, it also **sharpens** your focus on the things you consider important. Many psychological studies suggest that a **positive mindset** can lead to **positive outcomes** in life—this is another example of how the RAS influences our reality.

In later sections, we will discuss **behavioral awareness training**, where the RAS plays a critical role. We will explore the **hunter mindset**, which encourages us to constantly observe our environment. Developing a **heightened** awareness of the behaviors around us allows us to better understand situations from a **behavioral** standpoint.

It is important to recognize that **an eager and dedicated mindset** is the foundation for programming your RAS to be more effective at behavioral awareness. **Awareness is a choice.** It is **your** responsibility to make that choice and allow your mindset to guide your internal processes.

Having a Plan

Becoming an expert in **body language** and situational awareness requires **a plan**. Analyzing body language during an **active** interaction or while watching a video is relatively **easy**—in those cases, you are **focused** and have minimal distractions. However, maintaining **situational awareness** in real time requires more than just **reaction**—it demands **the right mindset**.

When reading the body language of a person you are **conversing with**, the goal is to recognize and understand their **reactions**. On the other hand, **reading** your environment is about recognizing and understanding the **mindsets** of those around you.

Behavioral awareness is about understanding the **behaviors** of those in your **vicinity**—whether they are passing you on a crowded street, sitting near you in a coffee shop, or loitering outside your home or workplace. In many cases, you may not have the **opportunity** to observe their reactions up close, but you **can** assess their **mindset**.

Training yourself to focus on **mindsets** and match them to the environment will help you identify what **fits** and what **does not fit** in a given situation. This skill will enable you to **spot outliers**—individuals who stand out because their behavior does not match their surroundings.

The key takeaway is that **you cannot focus on everything**. If I find myself standing on a busy street with **100 people** around me, I don't want to divide my attention equally among all of them. Instead, I want to **identify the 10 individuals** who stand out and **focus on them**.

What Causes Complacency?

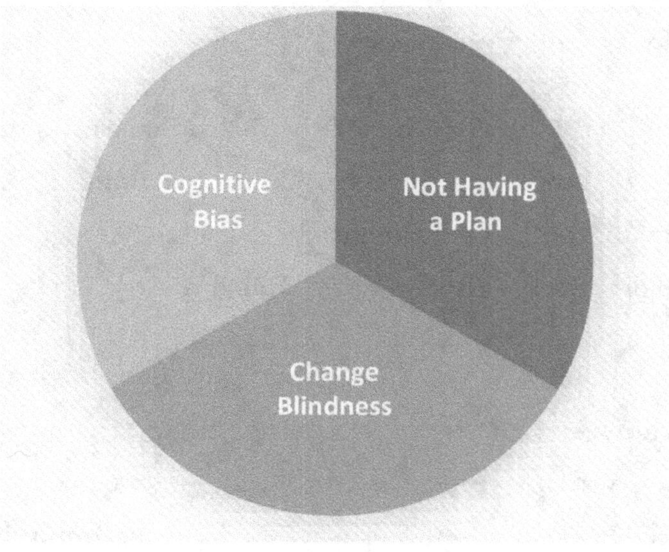

CHAPTER 2

Understanding Behaviors

The C.O.P ® Method for Understanding People

The study of body language and human behavior can be a long and detailed process. There is no shortage of books, articles, and websites that assign meanings to every movement or gesture people make. While this wealth of information is valuable, it can become overwhelming when a quick decision is needed.

For those who take their safety seriously, some decisions must be made quickly, requiring a simple yet effective approach. I have spent years studying body language and have found a more straightforward method. Many people are familiar with the phrase **"keep it simple, stupid"** or **KISS**. I have found this philosophy to be highly effective in my studies. When it comes to behavioral awareness, simplicity is essential because we may not have much time to react.

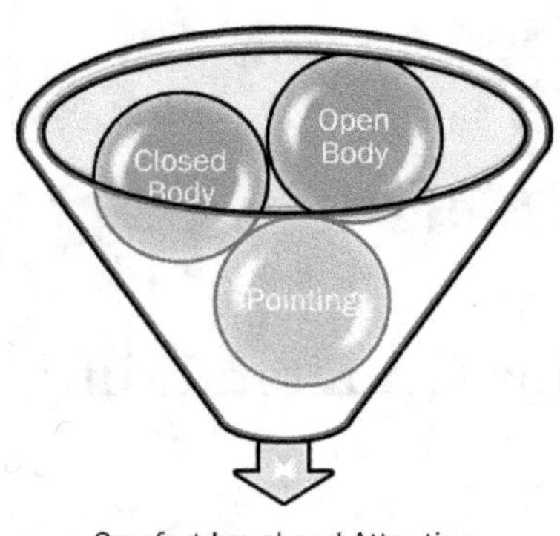

Comfort Level and Attention

In this book, you will learn to focus on basic human needs, wants, and desires to reduce the chances of being misled or deceived. This is why we begin with the **COP Method**, which serves as the foundation of this training course and will be referenced throughout the book.

The **COP Method** stands for **Closed, Open, and Pointing**—a framework used to assess **comfort levels** and **attention direction**. The next section will explore these behaviors and how they can help you better understand those around you.

Closed Body

We begin with closed body language, which consists of movements and gestures that indicate a need for protection. While it is obvious that we would feel a need for protection when facing a physical attack, we also instinctively react defensively in response to

Closed Body Language

- Closed gestures are a subconscious attempt to defend against the perceived situation.
- Defensive mindset Indicative of fear, suspicion, or dislike. Fear of an attack

emotional, verbal, or psychological threats.

The term attack in this context refers to anything that makes a person feel uncomfortable, fearful, or vulnerable, prompting a subconscious effort to shield or protect oneself. This response can be triggered by a variety of situations, from physical danger to social discomfort.

When people feel the need to protect themselves, they often do so by covering or shielding certain parts of their body. Common defensive gestures include crossing the arms, cupping the hands over the face, or closing the eyes. These actions serve as an instinctive barrier, providing a sense of security.

If someone is physically attacked, their natural reaction is to move their hands into a defensive position, either to block or redirect the incoming force and minimize injury. This protective instinct is not limited to physical threats; it also applies to emotional and psychological stress. When confronted with hurtful words, uncomfortable truths, fear of being caught in deception, or other vulnerabilities, a person may exhibit similar defensive movements.

These behaviors indicate discomfort and a desire to withdraw from the situation. When we recognize these signs in others, we can gain valuable insights into their emotional state and level of comfort.

- You are relaying a news report to a woman in your neighborhood about a man who has been accosting women at night. As she listens to you, she crosses her arms tightly across her chest and grips the collars of her shirt, signaling discomfort and concern.

- You are having a conversation with a coworker about a new workout routine you started and how you have lost 15 pounds in two months. Your coworker, who is overweight and known to have unhealthy eating habits, pulls his suit jacket closed, crosses his arms, and wipes his face near his mouth. His closed-off body language suggests that he may be feeling self-conscious or uncomfortable with the discussion.

Open Body

When someone exhibits open body language, they are making no effort to cover themselves or shield their body, signaling that they are comfortable, confident, and not expecting any form of attack. Open body language is commonly associated with feelings of relaxation, trust, and engagement.

These two concepts—open and closed body language—may seem simple, but they form two of the three fundamental building blocks of behavioral awareness. Recognizing these cues is essential for assessing a person's state of mind and determining whether they feel at ease or defensive in a given situation.

When someone displays open body language, it is often a sign that they are comfortable with their surroundings, willing to engage with others, and not experiencing fear or anxiety. In many cases, this posture indicates that they feel safe and unthreatened.

Understanding open body language is particularly useful when reading social interactions. A person with an open posture is more likely to be welcoming, engaged, and receptive to conversation. Conversely, if someone suddenly shifts from an open to a closed posture, it may indicate that they have become uncomfortable, defensive, or withdrawn.

Open Body Language

- Open gestures show an openness and comfort to their surroundings
- Open gestures are those that let down defenses
- They allow themselves to be open to attack because they are confident no attack is coming.

Later in the book, we will explore these concepts in greater depth, but for now, the goal is to observe body language and determine whether it appears open or closed.

- You have been asked by a close friend to watch their teenage son for a few hours. While trying to engage him in conversation, you notice that he has his arms and legs crossed and keeps glancing at the TV in the other room whenever there is a break in the conversation. However, when you ask him about the superhero character on his t-shirt, his eyes widen, his arms become animated, and he leans forward while speaking excitedly. This sudden shift in body language suggests that he is now comfortable and engaged in the conversation.

- You are at a popular nightlife venue and notice someone sitting across the bar who keeps glancing at you in a positive way. You decide to approach them and strike up a conversation. As you do, their eyes widen, they sit up straighter, and they move their glass to clear space for you. Their open body language suggests that they are interested in interacting with you and welcoming your presence.

By carefully observing body language in different social and professional settings, we can gain valuable insight into how people are feeling and reacting to their environment. The ability to distinguish between open and closed body language will serve as an essential skill throughout this book.

Open Behaviors	Closed Behaviors
Crossed Legs (Seated)	Crossed Arms
Visible Palms	Hands on Hips
Eyebrow Flash	Non-Visible Palms
Genital Exposure	Eyebrows Furrowed
Eye Contact	Closed Elbows
Elbows Out	Locked Ankles
Crossed Legs (Seated)	Pursed Lips
Visible Palms	Wrist Holding
Eyebrow Flash Genital Exposure Open Arms	Crossed Arms Hands on Hips Body Angled Away
Source: Behavioral Analysis Training Group	

Pointing Body

We point toward what we want, and it is just that simple. The human body's eight zones that can indicate where attention is directed are the head, eyes, shoulders, arms, hands, hips, knees, and feet. These zones respond to a person's mindset by pointing toward what is being thought about or desired.

If a person is talking to you but their feet are pointed toward the door, this could indicate a desire to leave. If you are having a conversation with someone who feels the need to exit, they might first point one foot toward the door, followed by a knee, and then begin glancing in that direction. Their shoulder and hip may also start shifting toward the door, as if their body is trying to move but is being held back by some obligation or hesitation. These cues suggest that their focus is on leaving the interaction.

Each of the eight zones should be observed individually, but the more signs of alignment you notice, the stronger the person's intent is.

- A police officer conducting a traffic stop notices that while speaking to the driver, the driver appears nervous and continuously glances toward a bag on the passenger seat.
- You are sitting at a table in a restaurant when you catch a person staring at you from across the room. At first, you think little of it and go about your meal, until you notice that their feet, knees, and hips are pointed in your direction.

Pointing Body Language
- The body will usually point itself toward what it wants.
- If a person is pointed toward the door, it may mean they want to walk through it.
- If pointed at a person or object, it usually indicates a desire to be around the person or object.

- A coworker is giving a sales presentation on a product you have little interest in. Suddenly, you remember that you forgot to submit an important report. As you anxiously check the time, your thoughts shift to the report sitting on your desk and your urgent need to leave the meeting to retrieve it.

As you picture these situations, consider how the body zones may have been pointing in specific directions as a direct reflection of a person's thoughts or desires at that moment.

8 Zones Of Pointing

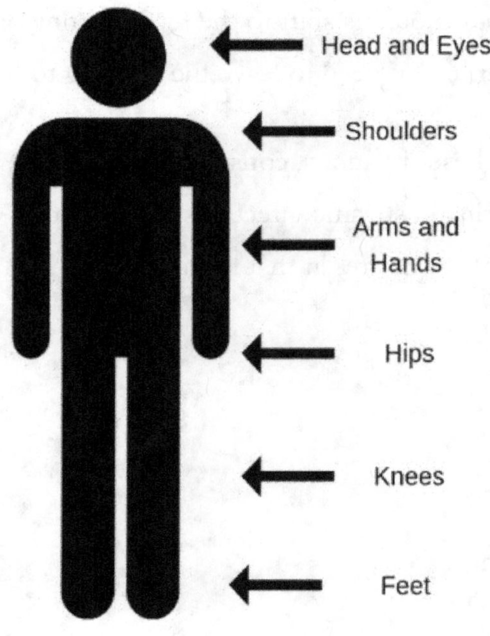

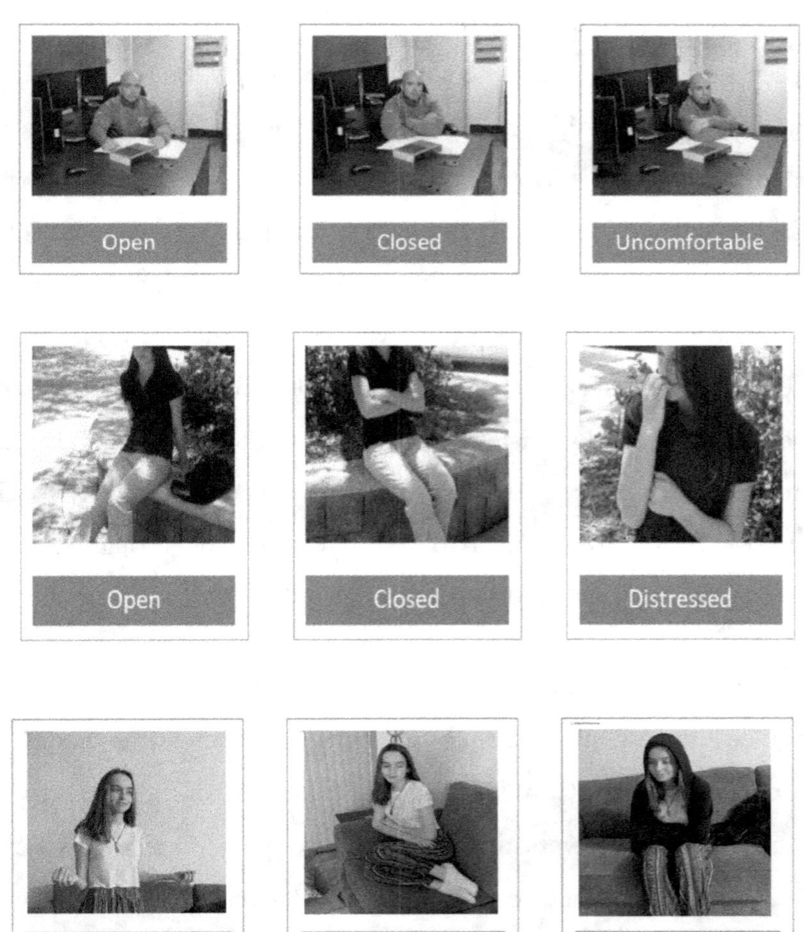

C.O.P is the body's way of showing comfort and attention.

Pointing Zone Conflict

When assessing someone's comfort level, you may find distinct parts of their body open while others are closed. Simply saying "look at the body language" may not always be as easy as it seems. For example, someone may display open body language with their arms and face while showing closed body language with their legs and feet. This inconsistency suggests **conflict**, meaning there is a dual mindset at play. The person may feel comfortable with part of the conversation but have underlying suspicions. They may also be unsure of what is expected, confused by what is being communicated, or even attempting to misrepresent their intentions. In the context of this study, conflict refers to the mind holding two or more opposing thoughts, which causes body language to react accordingly.

Imagine I am having a conversation with someone I respect and genuinely enjoy speaking with, but I have a meeting to attend and I am already running late. Conflict occurs because part of me wants to stay and continue the conversation, while another part of me knows I must leave. This creates what we often refer to as feeling "torn" between two choices. My body will reflect this by showing opposing thoughts—my upper body, including my eyes, shoulders, arms, and hands, will remain engaged in the conversation, but my lower body, including my feet, hips, and knees, may start pointing toward the door.

The body is very obedient to the messages sent by the brain. When the mind sends two different signals, the body reacts, and this is one of the main reasons we can read body language. Many times, a person's body language will contradict what they are verbally expressing, revealing their true intentions or state of mind.

C.O.P. for the Group Dynamic

When analyzing a group of people, the C.O.P. Method can still be applied because the same principles hold true. What can be observed in an individual can also be assessed within a group by looking not only at each person but also at their relation to the rest of the group. Since an individual's stance communicates their comfort level and mindset, the same applies to groups. By observing whether individuals within a group are open or closed and where they are pointing, we can gather valuable information about the group dynamic.

One important insight that can be gained from this observation is identifying who is in charge or who holds the highest status within the group. If active communication is taking place and most members are oriented toward a single person, this likely indicates that this individual has a level of influence or leadership. Another key takeaway is assessing how the group feels about their environment. The open or closed stance of the group as a whole can provide a clear indication of their collective comfort level.

A crucial factor in determining whether a group is open or closed is looking at the group as a whole. A group's overall stance conveys its mindset to outsiders. An open group will exhibit the characteristics of open individuals—members will appear comfortable with their surroundings, relaxed, and unconcerned with security or secrecy. They will be open in their communication and unlikely to show signs of anxiety. A closed group, on the other hand, will appear guarded, uneasy, and aware of their surroundings. Their posture will indicate concern or even secrecy, showing a level of discomfort with those outside the group.

It is not difficult to distinguish an open group from a closed one.

- You are sitting around a table in the break room with several coworkers, discussing a new restaurant that just opened in the neighborhood. Everyone is excited, actively engaging in conversation, and making plans to go as a group for happy hour and dinner on Friday.
- You are sitting around a table in the break room with several coworkers, discussing the same restaurant. However, this time, the discussion is in hushed tones because you are secretly planning a surprise birthday party for a coworker who is just outside the door talking to a client.

Putting It All Together

Imagine walking into a coffee shop and scanning the area as you pass through the door. In the back corner, you notice a group of three individuals engaged in open communication. Each member is displaying open body language, and their attention is directed toward each other or a central point in their conversation. Based on these observations, you judge that they are in a comfortable discussion among people they know well.

As you continue into the establishment, the group notices you. Each individual momentarily looks in your direction before quickly glancing back at each other. Moments later, you observe a shift in their body language. Their arms cross, their heads dip slightly lower, and their facial expressions change from open and casual to closed and serious. Their stance, which was previously relaxed, becomes tighter, with members standing closer together as if to shield themselves or their conversation.

In this moment, you have just witnessed a group dynamic shift from open to closed. If you are trying to assess whether this is something to be concerned about, consider the nature of an open versus a closed stance. Open body language indicates comfort with the surroundings, while a closed stance suggests the opposite. When this group changed its posture, it signaled a shift in mindset, indicating discomfort or unease with a change in their environment.

CHAPTER 3

THE BASIC COMMUNICATION MINDSETS

The mind and the body share a connection, and this is the reason we have body language. This connection is not a one-way street. We know that our mindset and mental processes travel down our nervous system and change the position of our body to reflect thoughts, attitudes, and reactions to our environment. However, it is also a little-known fact that this process works in reverse as well. The position of the body can, in certain ways, affect our mindset. While this does not mean that placing a very stubborn person in an open position will immediately make them agreeable, it does mean that doing so may give you a slight advantage in making them more receptive, which can lead to easier communication.

We are going to discuss the four basic mindsets that can be determined by someone's body positioning during communication. Body language is all about communication, and learning to recognize a person's mindset will aid in making interactions more effective.

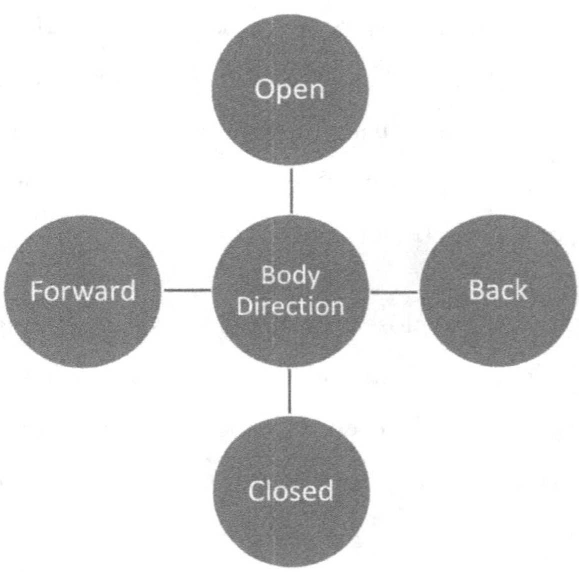

The four basic mindsets are responsive, contemplative, defensive, and aggressive.

- Responsive indicates that someone is open to communication and willing to engage.
- Contemplative suggests the person is considering what is being communicated or weighing the circumstances at hand.
- Defensive means the person feels vulnerable or exposed and wants to protect themselves.
- Aggressive indicates a person has the urge to lash out or become argumentative.

The following diagram represents the basic body language descriptions previously covered in this book. Open and closed refer to body positioning and show whether a person is comfortable with their surroundings or feeling guarded. Forward and backward positioning indicate whether a person is leaning in, showing interest in the interaction, or leaning back to create distance.

1. A forward and closed position suggests an aggressive mindset.
2. A forward and open position suggests a responsive mindset.
3. A backward and closed position indicates a defensive mindset.
4. A backward and open position indicates a contemplative mindset.

While these may seem simple, they can be particularly useful when engaging in communication. Imagine you are in the following scenarios and identify the mindset reflected in the body language.

- A person in a conversation is passionately debating a political stance.
- A loan officer at a bank listens to a customer's pitch for a new business loan, then reclines in his chair, puts his hands behind his head, and stares at the ceiling.
- A spouse being confronted with accusations of infidelity sits with their arms crossed knees together, and leans back in their chair.

- A brand-new employee sits in their boss's office, eager to learn about their new job. Their hands are neatly folded in their lap, their eyes are wide, and they lean forward to ensure they hear every word.

Answers: 1, 4, 3, and 2.

While this may seem like a useful trick for determining how someone is feeling during a conversation, it has the potential for a much deeper and more practical application. One aspect of behavioral awareness is recognizing surveillance behaviors. This book will introduce different ways to assess those around you and your environment.

If you are sitting in a public place and wondering whether someone is watching you, you may struggle to notice it by simply looking at an outdoor café across the street, where tables are filled with people enjoying their meals. At first glance, it may not seem like you are gaining much insight into behavioral awareness just by observing people casually talking over food. This assumption is likely correct—two people sharing a pizza a block away probably do not require your attention. However, is that always the case?

When observing people at an outdoor café, it is important to distinguish between genuine conversations and those who may be pretending to be engaged while actually paying attention to you. Using the COP Method, you can analyze where people are pointing, whether they are open or closed, and apply the mindset training you just learned to assess their interactions.

Now, let us take this a step further.

Consider the types of conversations happening in the café. You observe two people sitting at a table. One has an aggressive mindset, while the other appears defensive. Or perhaps one person is defensive while the other is contemplative. What types of discussions or topics might lead to these dynamics?

- A father and son are sitting at a table facing each other. The father is clearly upset that his son has failed to maintain his GPA at the university, causing him to lose his student aid scholarship. The son, realizing the financial burden he has placed on his father—who will now have to cover full tuition—tries to explain how he plans to work harder next semester and take on a part-time job.

- Two men sit across from each other at a table. One is explaining that he did not mean to contact his ex-girlfriend and that his current girlfriend has found out, putting his relationship in jeopardy. His friend is sitting across from him, thinking of ways to help him repair the situation.

These examples should look familiar. The first represents an aggressive-defensive dynamic, while the second represents a defensive-contemplative dynamic.

CHAPTER 4

Understanding People and the Environment: Viewing the Mindsets Around us

Part of the reason we look toward body language is to understand what is being communicated and to determine where people's interests lie.

We learned in the C.O.P. section that we tend to point toward what we are interested in or what we want to be around us. This could be a conversation, a person, an object, or a geographic area. In short, it is about interest. A person's interest can be conveyed by a series of simple indicators, such as how they sit, where they point, and what they have around them. Understanding the body language associated with interest will greatly enhance our situational awareness regarding surveillance.

Indicators that someone has an interest in something are recognized by where their body is leaning and pointing. This will indicate what their mind is concentrated on. Likewise, the body will be open and responsive, with limited stress, reducing unnecessary movements such as fidgeting or bouncing feet. There may also be facial indicators, including a tilted head or squinted eyes, if mental effort is involved in the observation.

Interest

The interest and disinterest of those around you can have significant importance for your awareness. As we observe people, we seek to match their behaviors to what the environment prescribes. A person sitting at a café table reading a newspaper may be perfectly normal and non-threatening. However, if a quick check of their body language shows that their feet, legs, hips, arms, and eyes are all pointed at the jewelry store across the street while only holding the book with their hands, what does that indicate about their interest and disinterest? There is a disinterest in the book and an interest in the business. The interest may be temporary, such as if the person's wife is in the store, but it is still important to recognize that there is interest.

Interest:
This position shows that individuals feels vulnerable or exposed by the situation and wishes to protect themselves.

If you are walking in a downtown area next to a small park in a restaurant district of a nearby city, you may notice a woman sitting at a park table reading a magazine. However, her feet, knees, and shoulders are pointed at a café across the street, where a man and a woman are sitting at a table out front. The book, arms, and head that she is reading are slightly off-center in a different direction. From time to time, she picks her head up from the book, looks around, and then glances at the café before lowering her head again.

Disinterest

When someone is disinterested in something, they may exhibit intensive fidgeting behaviors, such as bouncing feet, which indicate a desire or preparation to leave or walk away. This will be accompanied by anxiety cues, such as fidgeting, shifting movements, or placing objects in front of them as a barrier. This is usually observed when someone is seated at a table with accessible items. Their body language may be conflicted, especially in terms of where their body zones are pointing. This can suggest distraction or uncertainty about where to focus attention. These cues are different from a neutral feeling of simply "not caring" about a person, place, or thing. Instead, they are active cues of disinterest that border on avoidance.

If you are casually walking down the street in a busy commercial district of a nearby city and see a person sitting across the street in a vehicle, you may casually make eye contact as you pass. If the person does not meet your gaze but instead raises their phone closer to their face and shifts their body away from you at that moment, this is a strong indicator of disinterest.

Comfortable

Body language is about understanding communication, and many times, it is not the communication someone wishes you to see. As mentioned in an earlier chapter, body language is the physical manifestation of what is going on in the mind. A feeling of comfort or discomfort is one of the most basic emotions and, therefore, one of the easiest to identify.

Indicators that someone is feeling comfortable are related to interest and low anxiety. Their body zones will be pointed toward the point of interest if one is present. Their posture will be open, free of protective measures or covering. Their feet will be relaxed and possibly crossed, as there is no immediate need to leave. Anxiety

Comfortable with Surroundings

- No/low stress response
- Pointed toward interest
- Positive Proximity (Distance)
- Open gestures
- Open facial expressions
- Relaxed affect
- Calm movements

indicators will be nearly nonexistent, and unnecessary movements will be rare.

Uncomfortable

Indicators that someone is feeling uncomfortable or anxious are based on signs of distress and the desire to leave. You will notice that their feet may bounce and become restless, indicating their urge to leave. Their body will exhibit closed body language, such as crossed legs and arms. Their body zones will point away, directing toward a location that feels more comfortable. Anxiety

Uncomfortable with Surroundings

- Conflicted Pointing
- Closed Body language
- Protective Body Language
- Moderate stress response
- Raised Shoulders
- Negative proximity
- (Distance)
- Increased blinking
- Making a fort
- Choppy movements

behaviors will be more frequent, and countering behaviors, such as self-soothing and deep breaths, will be evident. They may also engage in physical protective measures, such as covering exposed areas of the body that feel vulnerable or placing objects between themselves and others as if to create a barrier.

Dominant

A dominant mindset is free of anxiety or discomfort regarding its surroundings. The body language will reflect a take-charge and sometimes intrusive nature. When sitting, the body will spread out to take up space, which is referred to as an expansive gesture. This may be directed toward others by occupying space that would typically belong to someone else. Their eyes and pointing zones will be directed toward what they want.

If  

standing, their posture will be upright with confident gestures, such as placing hands on their hips or other attention-getting stances. This person may touch others in one of two ways. The first is similar to that of a coach, involving pats on the back, the head, or other gestures that indicate enthusiasm and motivation. The second involves rough pats on the back, overly firm handshakes designed to intimidate, or forcing others to accommodate their movements. A dominant mindset may also lead to ignoring others in social situations.

Submissive

A submissive mindset means a person is fearful of something, either in their presence or in their surroundings. They will usually attempt to make themselves appear smaller and avoid drawing attention. Their body language will be closed yet non-threatening. They may clutch items close to their chest or wrap their legs around the legs of a chair. Their eyes will display a "help me" look, characterized by wide-open eyes and raised eyebrows. The primary motivation for those in this mindset is to remain unnoticed and avoid conflict.

> **Submissive Mindset**
> - Closed Gestures
> - Posture that attempts to make themselves smaller
> - Clutching items
> - Wide eyes and raised eyebrows

Protective

A protective mindset arises when someone feels the need to seek refuge from their environment or

> **Protective Mindset**
> - Closed Gestures
> - Covering genitals, breasts, etc.
> - Raised shoulders and self-holding
> - Darting glances
> - Hand(s) in Pocket

someone within it. This may manifest in closed gestures such as crossed arms, raised shoulders, or self-holding. They may also cover areas of the body that feel especially vulnerable, such as the genitals, chest, or other sensitive regions. Darting glances are common, and if they are walking, their stride and movement will likely fluctuate to reflect their anxiety.

Unprotected

An unprotected mindset is demonstrated by open body language and low anxiety in proximity to others. Their posture will be more dominant and comfortable, with movements that are consistent rather than shifting in direction or speed, as might be observed in a protective mindset.

Positive and Negative Proximity

Positive and negative proximity deal with a person's comfort level in close contact with others. This could involve sitting in a conversation, sharing a table, or walking through a crowded area. A person with a positive proximity

Positive Proxemics:
This mindset allows the individual to have to anxiety of people in close proximity to them.

mindset is unconcerned with the presence of others and how they interact. An example of this would be someone moving through a crowded environment with ease.

A person with a negative proximity mindset will feel uncomfortable when others are near. For instance, someone in an unfamiliar crowd may show signs of anxiety. They may draw their arms closer to their sides, glance around frequently, or display protective gestures.

Familiar with Surroundings

Recognizing whether someone is familiar with their surroundings can provide insight into whether they are a regular in the area or a visitor. A person unfamiliar with their environment may display darting glances, wide eyes, and raised eyebrows, suggesting they are seeking help or feeling lost. Their stride may be erratic, indicating uncertainty.

In contrast, a person who is familiar with their surroundings will walk at a confident, steady pace. Their eyes will not display a "help me" expression, and they will not exhibit frequent darting glances if they feel safe. Their body language may be neutral or even closed, signaling no need for assistance.

We can clearly see the differences in behavior when someone is familiar with their surroundings.

Understanding these mindsets is a crucial aspect of behavioral awareness. The ability to recognize not only these postures but also changes in body language will enhance situational awareness, allowing for a deeper understanding of the environment and the intentions of those within it.

CHAPTER 5

Aggression, Strength, Weakness, Submission

This mindset is a perception of one's self derived from several different situational and environmental factors. It is important to remember that the environment is fluid and ever-changing, influenced by any number of factors. A mindset can change drastically with these changes, so it is important to understand the basis for mindsets as well as their behavioral cues.

The first factor we will explore is the self-confidence one has in the current environment. This includes the individual's perception of their ability to "handle themselves" in that environment. This is not always a physical security aspect, although it can be. It also includes the ability to converse with others effectively, contribute to the environment, be knowledgeable in the subject at hand, or simply feel as if they fit in. In plain terms, this refers to the individual's comfort level in the environment. That comfort level is influenced by their reason for being in the environment or how the environment has developed in relation to them.

We will examine four factors that involve mindset within the interpersonal and environmental context. These four factors are aggression, strength, weakness, and submission. These factors represent mindsets commonly found in interpersonal communication or in a person's reaction to a specific environmental stimulus. When analyzing these mindsets, we must also consider how they manifest through body language and how they are formed in order to improve our ability to communicate effectively. Many of these mindsets can be observed from a distance, making them another useful tool for situational awareness.

Understanding the mindsets of those around us provides insight into their intentions, allowing us to prepare ourselves and avoid being caught off guard. It also helps us recognize when no threat is present. Additionally, this understanding enhances our ability to articulate why we did or did not act in a certain situation.

The following are five examples of some of the reasons behind certain mindsets. We will discuss each of these and relate them to the behaviors outlined in the table. While this is not a definitive or all-encompassing list, it provides insight into how to begin analyzing people's mindsets.

Self-Confidence:

Self-confidence is a mindset that reflects how we feel about a situation. As discussed earlier, being able to "handle ourselves" in the current environment plays a role in this. Self-confidence exists on a scale ranging from high to low, and our perception of ourselves influences our body language accordingly. A higher level of self-confidence results in strength, and our gestures and body language will reinforce this mindset. Conversely, a lower level of self-confidence results in weakness or even submission.

Self-Consciousness:

Self-consciousness is a mindset associated with inadequacy. When we are self-conscious, we experience self-doubt regarding how we will handle a situation. In many cases, we are also acutely aware of how others perceive our response to the situation. Often, we attempt to conceal this mindset from others, but it still manifests in our body language.

When reviewing the table, self-consciousness aligns with behaviors associated with weakness and submission. From previous training, we know to look for indicators such as closed body language and pointing behaviors that signal discomfort with the environment and a possible desire to leave.

Fear:

Fear is a state that can affect even the most confident individuals and is rarely absent from someone's mindset. The human mind fears many things, but it is important to keep fear in perspective and recognize its varying levels.

In interpersonal conversations, fear does not necessarily mean fear of another individual or physical harm. Instead, it can manifest as hesitation or discomfort regarding the topic or potential outcomes of the conversation. This mindset may be expressed through aggression, weakness, or submission, depending on the circumstances.

Expectation:

An expectation mindset means that an individual enters an interpersonal exchange anticipating a gain. This gain could be material or a victory in a conversation.

A person with this mindset is likely to exude confidence and strength, as they believe they will emerge from the exchange in a stronger position. The greater the perceived gain, the more the body language may shift toward aggression or strength.

However, the opposite may also be true. If an individual enters an exchange expecting that they may not achieve their desired gain but still needs to try, they may exhibit behaviors associated with weakness or submission. This is particularly true when the gain is not earned but must be requested or begged for.

Mission:

A mission-oriented mindset belongs to someone who is dedicated and focused on achieving a specific outcome. In short, they are on a mission.

This mindset is generally associated with strength and, depending on the nature of the mission, may also lean toward aggression due to the high degree of self-confidence involved.

The following table outlines the four mindsets we have previously discussed. It illustrates how, when observing interpersonal behaviors and communication from a distance, one can assess the mindsets of those engaged in conversation.

When considering situational awareness, it is important to recognize that there may be times when we are under surveillance. Observing people from a distance requires an understanding of their mindset and the ability to link it to their communication within a group.

Understanding mindset and communication is crucial for recognizing counter-surveillance behaviors. When monitoring the environment and observing those around you, it is essential to assess not only their body language but also whether their purpose for being there aligns with the environment. Simply put, the goal is to determine whether their engagement in an activity is genuine or whether their body language suggests they are watching you or engaging in something contrary to what they appear to be doing.

These sections are designed to prepare you for situational awareness and counter-surveillance by helping you understand communication and interpersonal dynamics.

Aggression	Strength	Weakness	Submission
VERBAL CUES			
LOUD/YELLING	EVEN TONE	SOFT SPOKEN	LOW TALK
FORCEFUL WORDS	DEFINITIVE WORDS	JUSTIFYING	AVOIDANCE LANGUAGE
DEMANDING TONE	CONTROLLED TONE	CONVINCING TONE	AGREEABLE TONE
VULGAR	FIRM SPEECH	CAREFUL	CONFIRMATION
INSULTING	DIRECT	JUSTIFYING	COMPLIMENTARY
PHYSICAL CUES			
ATTENTION GESTURES	CONTROLLED GESTURES	CLOSED GESTURES	RAPID RESPONSES
CHIN THRUST	OPEN	POINTING/LEANING AWAY	LOWERED HEAD
PROXIMITY INVASIONS	RESPECTFUL DISTANCE	DISTANCING	ANXIETY
TENSE FACIAL MUSCLES			WEIGHT SHIFTS
			FEARFUL
EYE CUES			
TARGET GAZE/GLARING	DIRECT GAZE	DOWNWARD GLANCES	LIMITED EYE CONTACT
WIDE EYED	POSITIVE EYE CONTACT	PARTIAL EYE CONTACT	DARTING GLANCES
RAPID BLINKING	NORMAL BLINKING	WIDE EYES	
POSTURE			
INFLATED	OPEN	CLOSED	SLOUCHED
POSTURED	EVEN WEIGHT DISPLAY	SLOUCHING	

CHAPTER 6

Understanding Suspicious Behaviors

Suspicious Behaviors
Anxiety – concealing behaviors – escape and evasion
Understanding the SOR - sudden observation reaction

When you study suspicion, you must examine the context and situation as much as you study the behaviors. Suspicion is a mindset exhibited through body language. It does not arise solely from a set of circumstances; rather, it results from the mental attitude of the individual in a given situation. This is where context becomes crucial. Suspicious behavior is rooted in fear and the desire to remain undetected. If an individual has no apprehension about being discovered while engaging in a certain behavior, they are far less likely to exhibit body language associated with suspicious behavior.

This section will address the mindset and actions of those engaged in what we will describe as suspicious behaviors. Defining suspicious behaviors can be challenging because different contexts and situations can alter what constitutes suspicion and how we recognize it. For the purposes of behavioral awareness—understanding your surroundings and ensuring safety—we will define it as follows:

Suspicious behaviors are actions specifically intended to mask one's true intentions. These behaviors cause the individual anxiety, as they fear their true intentions will be discovered. It is essential to remember that suspicious behaviors are situational and must be analyzed alongside the context in which they occur.

This study will be divided into three basic categories of suspicious body language behaviors: anxiety, concealing, and escape.

Anxiety

Movements - Verbal Indicators - Mental Processes

The behaviors associated with anxiety can be numerous. You may already be aware of common anxiety-related behaviors such as fidgeting, involuntary movements, adjusting clothing, sweating, and changes in vocal tone or speech patterns. While there is significant variation in these behaviors, we will focus on those most likely to indicate anxiety in situations we consider suspicious.

When observing suspicious behavior, we typically look for actions that are designed to mask true intentions or to conceal the anxiety a person experiences while carrying out a certain task. We will concentrate on the behaviors most relevant to these situations.

Movements

When a person is anxious about being watched while performing a task, their body language will often change in noticeable ways. Consider what we have already learned about how body language shifts according to an individual's perception of their environment. If someone believes they are being observed and simultaneously fears being discovered while engaged in a certain activity, their movements will adjust to reflect this mindset. The mental processes at play will generate body language cues that reveal their anxiety.

We know that body language is a result of the body responding to thoughts in the brain. When observing behavior that seems suspicious, we use body language to uncover what the individual may be trying to hide.

If you were doing something wrong and believed you were being watched, it stands to reason that you would try to act in a way that makes you unnoticeable. People instinctively attempt to "act natural," but this often becomes their biggest downfall. During periods of high anxiety,

the brain does not make well-thought-out decisions (Lyle E. Bourne, 2003). Choosing behaviors is no exception. During these times, individuals are too distracted by their illicit act to be fully conscious of their body language. Since body movements are directly linked to thoughts, any attempt to suppress certain behaviors—such as fleeing, hiding, or concealing an object—creates a conflict. The mind struggles to maintain an appearance of normalcy, while the body involuntarily reacts to the stress.

For example, if someone is concealing an object beneath their clothing or in their pocket, they may experience anxiety about being discovered. As a result, their movements may appear stiff or unnatural. They may walk with an unusual rigidity, as though they are intensely focused on walking normally but are restricting certain body movements. Imagine someone walking while trying to balance an invisible book on their head. This exaggerated control over their body movements reflects their fear of exposing the concealed item.

A teenager attempting to hide a bottle of alcohol from his parents may loosen his pants and secure the bottle in his waistband, wearing a baggy shirt to cover it. He knows that as long as he remains still, the contraband will stay hidden. As he walks downstairs to leave the house, he moves stiffly, keeping his torso unnaturally rigid to avoid revealing the bottle's outline.

In another example, a suicide bomber walked into a police station in Kabul, Afghanistan, as captured by Al Jazeera TV footage. The man, wearing a dark suit, carried a folder as he made his way toward the police chief's office. Concealing an explosive vest beneath his jacket, he walked with an extremely rigid posture. His movements resembled those of someone wearing a back brace or carefully balancing an object on their head. Despite wearing a suit—common attire in police stations where officers frequently conceal weapons and ballistic armor—his rigid movements revealed his anxiety about being caught. Upon reaching the police chief's office, he detonated his explosive device.

Behavior Speed

When an individual is engaged in an activity where being discovered would not be beneficial, their anxiety may manifest in sudden changes in speed. A person may momentarily speed up while passing a security checkpoint and then slow down when they believe they are out of sight. This occurs because their mind urges them to minimize time in view, reducing the risk of detection. Once they believe they are safe, the anxiety subsides, and their movement returns to normal.

One morning, I was sitting in my patrol car completing paperwork near a public park and beach where alcohol was prohibited. A man and a woman walked past my car, each carrying a plastic travel mug. I initially paid little attention to them, but as the woman noticed my patrol car, she suddenly increased her walking speed. By the time she passed my car, the man she had been walking with was 20 feet behind her. His cup, now held at an angle, appeared to be empty. Her sudden change in behavior suggested she might have been concealing something, such as alcohol, in her cup.

If someone knowingly being observed slows their behavior, this can indicate intense concentration on appearing normal. The individual has become hyper-aware of being watched and is carefully measuring their movements to project an air of innocence. This hyper-awareness can create an unnatural stillness or exaggerated movements as they focus on controlling their body language.

Mental Processes

Anxiety and stress originate in the brain as reactions to environmental stimuli. These mental processes reveal themselves through various body language cues.

While we will discuss anxiety in different contexts throughout this book, in this section, we are focusing on anxiety as it relates to suspicious behavior. Individuals exhibiting suspicious behavior are often attempting to mask their actions and conceal their true intentions.

We are already familiar with physiological stress responses, including rapid eye blinking, avoiding eye contact, throat clearing, hand wringing, fidgeting, primping, or adjusting clothing. While these behaviors can stem from various causes, they are rarely exhibited by individuals under no stress. If we can reasonably rule out psychological or medical conditions, we can infer that the person is experiencing stress at the moment these behaviors occur.

To illustrate this concept, consider a simple teapot. When placed on a heat source, the water inside begins to boil, producing steam that exits through the spout, making a whistling sound. If you were to cover the spout with your finger, pressure would build inside the teapot. Eventually, the steam would either force its way out or remain trapped inside, testing the teapot's structural integrity.

This analogy mirrors how humans react under stress. Anxiety builds inside us like steam in a teapot. To relieve the pressure, we release small, involuntary behaviors such as fidgeting, adjusting our clothing, or nail-biting. If the anxiety remains contained, it will eventually manifest in larger, more noticeable ways.

1000-Yard Stare

When stress becomes unbearable or prolonged, the brain may attempt to shut down. This does not mean it ceases to function, but rather that it becomes overwhelmed, slowing cognitive abilities. Thought processes become impaired, decision-making deteriorates, and the body appears to operate on autopilot.

The term "1000-yard stare" describes the blank, emotionless gaze often observed in individuals experiencing extreme stress, particularly those exposed to prolonged trauma, such as combat. Their minds, exhausted by stress, appear disengaged from their surroundings.

If you observe someone exhibiting a 1000-yard stare, it is crucial to assess the context. This expression suggests that stress is paramount in their mind and is significantly affecting their behavior. Their ability to process external stimuli may be impaired, making them less responsive to their environment.

In the next section, we will further explore anxiety and how it translates into body language. Recognizing these behaviors is essential for understanding an individual's mental state and their potential intentions.

Surprise Facial Expression:	Anger Facial Expression:	Contempt Facial Expression:
• Wide Eyes • Eyebrows raised • Wrinkled forehead • Open mouth/ slack jaw	• The brows are lowered and drawn together • Vertical lines between the brows • Lower lid is tensed • hard stare • Lips can be pressed firmly • The lower jaw juts out	• Mouth drawn into a sneer • Possible sideways look • May see signs of anger also

Fear Facial Expression:	Disgust Facial Expression:	Frustration Facial Expression:
• Brows are raised and pulled together • Wrinkles in the forehead are in the center between the brows • Upper eyelid raised and lower lid is tense and raised • Upper eye has white showing on top of eye • Mouth is open and lips are slightly tensed or stretched and drawn back	• Wrinkled nose • Snarled lip • Lowered Brow • Slight head shake of look away • Upper teeth can be exposed • Raised cheeks	• Exhaled Lips • Sneer • Rolling the eyes • Looking away • Shaking head • Forced smile

Reactionary Body Movements

Reactionary movements are gestures that accompany a sudden reaction. These movements are typically related to pointing, protective gestures, or anxiety cues. They reflect a person's mindset—whether they want to move toward or away from a situation—or they may indicate feelings of anxiety or avoidance.

For example, imagine someone staring at an attractive person.

When that person looks back, the first reaction from the individual staring will usually be to quickly avert their gaze in a random direction. The same principle applies in surveillance situations. In the picture below, a person engaged in a surveillance operation is unsure where their target is and, as a result, shows unusual interest in a nearby plant while waiting.

In a similar instance, I witnessed a person conducting surveillance in a busy downtown area. The target unexpectedly turned toward the surveillance operator, catching them off guard and causing them to panic. The nearest object to them was a blue mailbox (pictured above). In response, the operator approached the mailbox, stared intently at the information card, and rubbed their hands along the sides as the target passed. This behavior drew the attention of not only the target but also several passersby.

The single most important factor in all three of these examples is the lack of a plan. Did the person in the bar have a plan for how to react when the attractive person returned their gaze? Did the surveillance operators have a plan for an unexpected encounter with their target? The answer is no, and that lack of preparation is the primary reason for their unnatural and revealing reactions.

Verbal Statements

You may have heard of the term "Freudian slip," which refers to when a person accidentally verbalizes something that is on their mind but was not intended to be said. This happens because they are dwelling on the thought, causing it to surface unexpectedly in their speech. The sudden observation reaction (SOR) can manifest in the same way through verbal statements.

We have learned that an initial reaction to a new stimulus in the environment may result in facial expressions, reactionary body movements, or verbal statements. The verbal statement SOR is defined as an immediate, spontaneous reaction—either spoken aloud or mouthed—in response to something new in the environment.

It is important not to overcomplicate this concept. It is simply a reflexive response in which a person reacts verbally without conscious thought. Here are a few examples:

- A loafing employee sees his boss enter the room and make eye contact with him. As he turns around, he mutters an expletive such as "Oh, shoot" in response to his boss entering the environment and its possible negative consequences.
- A person walking down the street holding a cup of coffee nearly collides with someone who accidentally steps in front of them. The person with the coffee instinctively says, "Oops."
- A driver notices a police officer behind them. When the officer's lights suddenly turn on, the driver utters an expletive under their breath.

These verbal statements are reflexive reactions to situations. If the person desires, they will quickly suppress or conceal their response within a few seconds.

The sudden observation reaction in body language is an essential tool for identifying an individual's first response to a change in their environment. Like all tools, it is not useful in every situation, but when observable, it provides a clear understanding of a person's perception of changes around them. Recognizing these cues allows for more effective communication and offers insight into a person's thought process, which can be used to your advantage.

CHAPTER 7

Understanding Violence

In this section, we will learn about the actions and mindset that lead to violence. This does not mean it will simply be a list of behaviors that equate to violence or its onset. Contrary to popular belief, people do not suddenly "snap" from a state of complete calm to an uncontrollable rage in the blink of an eye. Acts of violence are typically built upon experiences, circumstances, internal emotions, and reactions to the environment.

The process begins with an individual's initial perception of their surroundings, which, in many cases, is influenced by their comfort level. This can often be recognized through open or closed body language. It may then progress to determining one's motivation, which can be observed by noting where they are pointing. Are they seeking an escape route, or are they moving toward a perceived threat? Their body language may then develop into what we define as suspicious behavior, such as anxiety, concealing, or escape behaviors (ACE). These behaviors may indicate apprehension, an attempt to hide something, or a search for an exit. Violent encounters are built upon these behavioral building blocks.

Therefore, it is essential to keep in mind what you have previously learned about human behavior and understand that violence is rarely an instantaneous action.

With that in mind, we will now examine the actions that serve as preparations for violence. These include the mental shift from a non-violent state to contemplating violence and beginning the physiological process of preparing to carry it out.

Initial Realization

The initial realization occurs when a person either enters an environment or comes to the understanding that violence may be a possible outcome. At this early stage of comprehension, you are likely to see the COP Method in effect. This may begin with closed gestures and pointing toward avenues of escape, more comfortable environments, or a locked focus on an opponent. At this stage, the individual is still processing the situation and has not yet decided what action to take. They are merely becoming aware of the discomfort in their environment.

The opposite may also be true. In some cases, the realization of potential violence or danger may trigger aggressive behaviors. As a result, the individual's reaction may not be closed but rather open, though in a more dominant posture, with their body pointing directly at the perceived source of the threat.

Indicators of the initial realization may include:

- Closed gestures indicating discomfort or an uneasy mindset
- Negative proximity—maintaining distance from others
- Pointing toward a more comfortable environment or an exit
- Pointing at a perceived threat while adopting a dominant posture

The initial realization phase may also involve elements of the sudden observation reaction (SOR) or spontaneous verbal utterances. In these cases, the individual may say something that reflects their mindset but was not necessarily intended to be spoken aloud. Examples of these belief statements include: "I can't go back to jail," or "I knew it." These statements or gestures may indicate surrender, defiance, or non-compliance.

Decision-Making Process

The body language associated with the decision-making process reveals that a person is evaluating a situation. Accurately assessing this period is essential, as it allows for an inventory of the situation and environment to determine all aspects influencing the person's choices. The following cues indicate that an individual is actively making a decision:

- Stroking the face
- Tilting the head

- Squinting the eyes
- Averting the gaze or looking around
- Adjusting their stance
- Thrusting the chin forward

Physiological Reactions as the Body Prepares for Physical Exertion

When a person anticipates either fighting or fleeing from a situation, their body will instinctively react by initiating an adrenaline dump. This surge of adrenaline provides the necessary energy for rapid movement or combat. However, if the individual does not immediately utilize this energy, it can result in noticeable physiological responses. These responses may manifest as anxiety, fear, or heightened physical tension.

Common physiological reactions include:

- Shallow breathing, as the body compensates for the adrenaline surge
- Flaring nostrils, indicating an attempt to take in more oxygen
- Unnecessary movements such as fidgeting, bouncing feet, or a clenched jaw, signaling rising anxiety and blood pressure (similar to the "teapot effect")
- Dilated pupils as the eyes adjust to heightened alertness

Actions Associated with the Mind's Preparation for Violence

Once a person has determined that violence is imminent, their mind will begin developing a plan to respond to the threat. This mental preparation will translate into physical behaviors that anticipate violence or indicate an impending physical attack.

Common behaviors include:

- Blading the body or assuming a stance that enhances balance or protects vital areas
- Clenching hands or fingers into fists, reflecting mental preparation for striking
- Stretching joints or muscles, such as rolling the neck, loosening the shoulders, or shifting the knees
- Clenching the jaw
- Shifting body weight into a fighting stance
- Averting the eyes to scan the surroundings or conceal intent

Mindset Associated with Fleeing from Violence

Not every violent situation results in a fight—sometimes, fleeing is the better option. When an individual is contemplating escape rather than confrontation, their body language will reflect this internal decision. Many of the same principles from the COP Method apply, such as body orientation toward an exit, allies, or alternative solutions.

Indicators of an individual preparing to flee include:

- Pointing or angling their body toward an escape route or an ally
- Rapid, shallow breathing
- Darting glances in search of an exit
- Restless feet, preparing for sudden movement
- High anxiety, often visible through trembling or increased sweating
- Increased talkativeness, possibly as a nervous response

Mindset Indicating Focus and Intent

- Eyes locked onto a specific target
- Hand movements or subtle twitches indicating readiness to act
- The majority or all body zones pointing toward the target

Misdirection Actions Intended to Gain an Advantage

- Using calming gestures with the hands to mask intentions
- Focusing the gaze on unnecessary directions or objects to divert attention
- Making gestures or movements that suggest the presence of a weapon
- Closing the gap and moving closer while attempting to gain trust
- Combining non-compliance with clarifying questions to stall or assess the situation

It is important to remember that these gestures, cues, and movements are all indicative of a mindset. In this case, the mindset is the contemplation of violence. This means that violence is still in the planning stage and can potentially be de-escalated or redirected if one party makes a conscious decision to change the course of events.

Recognizing these pre-violence indicators does not guarantee the avoidance of conflict, but it does provide the opportunity to position yourself advantageously. Observing these behaviors allows you to understand when someone is actively contemplating violence, giving you a critical moment to act in a way that best suits the situation.

This could involve initiating a preemptive strike, creating distance to utilize a defensive tool or weapon, or escaping the scene before the situation escalates. There is no universally "right" or "wrong" response—what matters is that you recognize these cues in time to make the best decision for the given circumstances.

At the very least, detecting these gestures early allows you to mentally and physically prepare for a confrontation, reducing the likelihood of being caught off guard and significantly increasing your chances of survival and success.

CHAPTER 8

Situational Awareness: Assessing the Environmental baseline

Situational awareness is a term that is commonly used yet often misunderstood. The fundamentals of situational awareness are not difficult to practice, but the key challenge lies in making it a lifestyle rather than treating it as a training scenario or class exercise. Many times, people reference fictional spies from movies who notice every detail of every person, place, and object they encounter. While this is often portrayed as the pinnacle of situational awareness, it is usually not a realistic goal or even particularly useful in most situations.

For the purposes of this training, situational awareness consists of understanding the behaviors within a specific geographic area and those who occupy it. This understanding, combined with a mindset of continuous observation, will enable you to protect yourself and others. In this training, the term "situational awareness" will more accurately be referred to as "behavioral awareness."

This book focuses on understanding intentions and mindset because these are the driving forces behind people's actions. In the study of body language, you will frequently hear the term "baseline." This refers to the norm for a particular person, situation, or environment during a given period. When assessing a person's baseline, you are looking for common attributes and characteristics that the individual exhibits under normal circumstances in that environment. The same principle applies to the baseline of a geographic area.

A simple example of a personal baseline would be observing how often someone engages in unnecessary movements such as checking the time, scratching their face, or looking around. You would also assess their body language to determine their mood—are they relaxed, uncomfortable, or defensive? The reason for establishing a baseline is to compare it against the norm of the surrounding environment. By gauging an individual's mindset and identifying changes, you can recognize shifts in behavior. A change in one element of the baseline signals a shift in mindset, which requires further investigation.

For example, if you are observing someone whose baseline suggests they are relaxed, but you suddenly notice their body language shifting to discomfort, this indicates a new mindset. In the study of body language, the goal is to recognize these baseline changes so that an individual's mental state becomes clearer to us.

It is important to note that you do not need to observe a person for an extended period to establish a baseline. Every encounter has a baseline, and it may only take a few seconds to a few minutes to notice. Learning these observation methods will enhance your ability to understand the people around you.

We will now discuss baselines in relation to geographic areas or environments. As you enter a new environment, your first step is to scan the area and establish a baseline for assessment. Begin by asking yourself how the environment makes you feel. Is it neat, orderly, and stress-free? Or is it unkempt, dirty, and possibly dangerous? These are two extreme examples, but they provide a starting point for analyzing your surroundings. Most environments will fall somewhere in between. The goal is to develop an awareness of your surroundings from a behavioral perspective.

Let's imagine that you enter a neighborhood and find it disorganized and possibly unsafe. Your next step is to determine the baseline behavior of the people in this environment. Based on the conditions, you might expect individuals in this area to exhibit signs of discomfort and self-protection. From previous lessons, we know that some signs of discomfort include closed body language, avoidance of others, conflicted pointing, anxiety, raised shoulders, and negative proximity. While this may not always be the case, making these deductions allows you to develop a plan for situational awareness.

When assessing environments and establishing a baseline, it is crucial to understand the various types of environments you are analyzing and what composes them. You must consider the social makeup, infrastructure, and typical behaviors of people in these settings. These factors contribute to the psychology of how an environment functions. By understanding these elements, you will be able to recognize variations in the baseline.

These variations often manifest as individuals whose behavior does not align with the norms of the environment. While this does not necessarily indicate a threat, it does suggest that the individual has a different mindset than those around them. Such individuals may display actions and mindsets that are inconsistent with their surroundings, making them stand out.

For example, imagine you are sitting in an airport concourse, waiting for your plane to board in about 30 minutes. The waiting area near the boarding gates is crowded with other passengers in the same situation. From your vantage point, you can see six other boarding areas, each filled with a similar number of people. As you observe your surroundings, you assess that the normative behavior in this environment is relaxed and comfortable. Most people are engaged with electronic devices, books, or conversations. Aside from the general aggravation of waiting, the majority of passengers appear comfortable in their surroundings.

Now, consider what types of behavior might seem out of place in this environment. It is important to recognize that each airport will have its own set of behaviors depending on the situation. An airport experiencing massive delays will have a vastly different baseline than one with smooth and efficient operations.

When analyzing an environment and seeking to establish a baseline, you must also take into account the overall context of the situation. Profiling describes the attributes of various environments, and we will use these attributes to determine the expected body language of people in each setting. By understanding these norms, we can identify individuals whose behavior deviates from the expected baseline and determine whether further observation is necessary.

The table below will help you match environments with expected behaviors and identify behaviors that stand out as unusual.

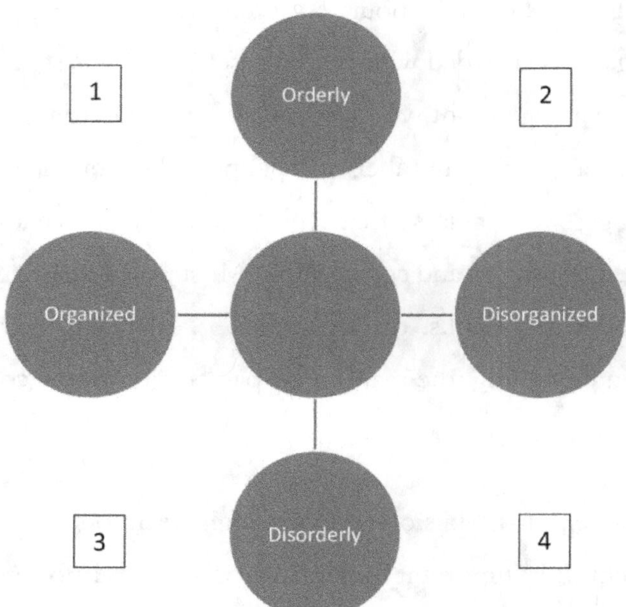

Environmental Behavior Baseline Table – Behavioral Analysis Training Group 2018

On the horizontal axis, we begin with the degree of socialization within an environment. On the left, we see a high level of social order, and on the right, we see a low level of social order or disorder. A high social order refers to areas where the inhabitants understand and abide by the established social structure.

An example of such an environment would be a middle-class neighborhood where one or two members of each household work, children attend school, and neighbors generally know one another. The houses, streets, and parks are well-maintained and clean, with few instances of street crime. Another example could be a commercial shopping district that is well lit, well-organized, and relatively crime-free. While one of these environments is a static residential area where the same people live, and the other is a transient space where people come and go, both are characterized by strong social organization.

Another example of a highly organized neighborhood would be an ethnic enclave in a major city, such as Little Italy in New York. While such neighborhoods may not always be affluent, they maintain a strong sense of social order. Families know each other, and social standing is both recognized and respected within the community. The prevalence of common street crime is lower due to long-standing family ties and the familiarity that residents have with one another.

At the other end of the spectrum is social disorder. A prime example would be a low-income housing development where graffiti covers the walls, and open-air drug dealing and prostitution occur on street corners. In such neighborhoods, high crime is an expected part of daily life, and residents navigate the streets with the awareness of either being victimized or victimizing others. These environments lack a strong sense of communal order.

Another example of a socially disorganized environment would be a highly transient neighborhood where residents do not develop personal ties, rarely know their neighbors, and make little or no effort to create a sense of community.

On the vertical axis, we begin at the top with orderly environments and descend toward disorderly ones. This axis represents the level of effort put into maintaining the physical aspects of the environment.

At the top end of the spectrum, we might see a well-manicured residential neighborhood or a commercial district that is kept neat and clean. At the disorderly end, we may find decaying neighborhoods where neither the government nor residents make an effort to maintain infrastructure. We might also see industrial areas that, while functional, lack any attempt at aesthetic improvement.

These areas influence the mindset of their inhabitants, primarily because people are there either out of necessity (e.g., employment) or because they reside there. While most areas we travel to are not at the extreme ends of the spectrum, they may share characteristics of these extremes, giving us insight into the behaviors and mindsets we can expect in those areas.

Now that we have reviewed the characteristics of environments, it is

important to understand that many aspects of an environment have yet to be explored. We are focusing on the base behaviors of a given environment so that we can align our expectations with the mindset typically found there. For example, an industrial area is considered a disorderly environment, as it prioritizes function and productivity over aesthetics. In such an environment, we would typically expect to see individuals who work there or have business in the area. The usual inhabitants would likely be comfortable in close proximity to each other and focused on their tasks. However, a flagged behavior in this setting might be someone who appears uncomfortable, exhibits signs of needing protection, or shows unfamiliarity with the area. While this does not automatically indicate illicit behavior, it does suggest a mindset that is inconsistent with the norm.

When profiling a neighborhood or new environment, we must identify the baseline behaviors of the area. If we cannot establish this baseline and find ourselves surrounded by 100 people, we would have to observe all 100 individuals. However, by determining the typical behaviors in that environment and identifying behaviors that deviate from the norm, we can narrow our focus significantly. The purpose of searching for behaviors outside the norm is to simplify the task of identifying anomalies while reinforcing the fact that we are not merely searching for threats or suspicious  activity. Instead, we are observing people and interpreting their communication, whether verbal or through body language.

For instance, imagine you are standing guard outside a government building in a large urban area, encountering thousands of people each day. Attempting to anticipate which of them might pose a threat is a daunting and exhausting task. Profiling your environment is a valuable tool that allows you to establish a baseline mindset for the area and identify those exhibiting flagged behaviors—behaviors that contradict the expected norm.

It is important to recognize that mindset is only one part of the equation. While it is a crucial factor in our observations, mistakes can easily be made. Suppose you are working as a security officer in an airport and have determined that the baseline behaviors in this environment include comfort with unfamiliarity and positive proximity to others. If you identify an individual who exhibits signs of discomfort, negative proximity, and high anxiety, this does not necessarily indicate an immediate threat. Instead, you have identified someone whose mindset contradicts the norm, warranting further observation or additional investigation, but not immediate alarm. This person may have an intense fear of flying, or they may be planning illicit behavior. It is essential to remember that these guidelines are merely tools for identifying behaviors that warrant closer scrutiny, rather than definitive indicators of wrongdoing.

In many cases, alert individuals may notice mindsets and behaviors that seem out of place but fail to react. One reason for this inaction is the inability to articulate what specific behaviors should be watched for, making them less likely to take action. Another reason is the absence of an active, watchful mindset, which allows cognitive biases—such as normalcy bias and change blindness—to interfere with noticing these behaviors. The exercise below provides examples of how an Environmental Baseline Profile should be structured.

Environment	Example	Expected Behavior	Flagged Behavior
ORDERLY	CLEAN, WELL-CARED FOR, LOW CRIME	COMFORTABLE	UNCOMFORTABE
DISORDERLY	DECAYING, NOT CARED FOR, CIGH CRIME	UNCOMFORTABE	COMFORTABLE
SOCIALLY ORGANIZED	GOOD SOCIAL STRUCTURE AND INTERNAL CONTROLS	COMFORTABLE, POSITIVE PROXIMITY,	UNCOMFORTABLE, UNFAMILIAR
SOCIALLY DISORGANIZED	NO SOCIAL STRUCTURE OR INTERNAL CONTROLS	UNCOMFORTABLE, PROTECTIVE, NEGATIVE PROXIMITY, ANXIETY	COMFORTABLE, UNFAMILIAR, UNPROTECTED
ORDERLY/ SOCIALLY ORGANIZED	UPPER CLASS, LOW CRIME NEIGHBORHOD	COMFORTABLE, FOCUSED, POSITIVE PROXIMITY	UNCOMFORTABLE, PROTECTIVE, ANXIETY
ORDERLY/ SOCIALLY DISORGANIZED	COMMERCIAL, MALL, URBAN SHOPPING DISTRICT	COMFORTABLE, UNFAMILIAR, POSITIVE PROXIMITY	UNCOMFORTABLE, PROTECTIVE, NEGATIVE PROXIMITY
DISORDERLY/ SOCIALLY DISORGANIZED	HIGH CRIME, LOW INCOME NEIGHBORHOD	UNCOMFORTABLE, PROTECTIVE, NEGATIVE PROXIMITY, ANXIETY	DOMINANT, POSITIVE PROXIMITY
DISORDERLY/ SOCIALLY ORGANIZED	INDUSTRIAL, GANG CONTROLLED AREA	UNCOMFORTABLE, PROTECTIVE, NEGATIVE PROXIMITY, ANXIETY	COMFORTABLE, UNFAMILIAR

Environmental Baseline Exercise

Exercise #1

- **Label the environment according to the table above:** The neighborhood is **orderly and organized** and appears to be a commercial downtown area.

- **Identify expected behaviors:** The inhabitants appear relaxed, exhibit **positive proxemics**, have an **unprotected mindset**, and are familiar with the area.

- **Establish flagged behaviors:** Protected mindset, **negative proxemics**, **concealing behaviors**, and **evasion** (sight patterns indicating a search for escape routes, foes, friends, etc.).

Exercise #2

- **Label the environment according to the table above:** This is an **enclosed or underground parking structure**. The vehicles suggest **short-term or daily storage**.

- **Identify expected behaviors:** The inhabitants will exhibit the following mindsets: **familiarity with surroundings** and a **mission mindset**, unless they do not remember where they parked, in which case they may display confusion or hesitation. Depending on the **area or time**, behaviors may also be **protective**, with **fast movements indicating anxiety**.

- **Establish flagged behaviors: Unprotected mindset used to fake calm, negative proxemics, concealing behaviors,** and **slow movements indicating a desire to remain unseen.**

Exercise #3

Test yourself

1. Label the environment according to the table above:

2. Identify expected behaviors:

3. Establish flagged behaviors:

CHAPTER 9

Putting it all together

The goal of this book and this type of training is to enhance our understanding of what is happening around us. **Mindset is always the key element, and knowledge is secondary.** Upon completing this book, you may feel as if you are ready to be "one with your environment" and prepared for anything. However, do not be misled by this thinking. **Behavioral awareness is a mindset that must be practiced until it becomes second nature.** Without consistent practice, its usefulness will be limited. On a positive note, developing this mindset is not difficult. The key to beginning this process is having a **plan** and implementing it into your daily routines. As you start integrating environmental awareness into your habits rather than treating it as a situational effort, use the following aspects of this book as a guide:

- Our environment serves as a guide to the types of **mindsets** and **behaviors** we expect to encounter. **Variations from the expected should not immediately be treated as suspicious** until they cannot be explained. Once we establish the norm for our environment, we shift our focus to how its inhabitants behave.

- Next, we turn our attention to **the focus of those around us.** Our **attention should always be on what their attention is on.** This is where **conflicted body language** becomes significant, as many of the most revealing cues come from people trying to conceal their true focus. **The biggest determining factor will be the eight zones of pointing,** combined with potential contradictions in body language.

- At this stage, we analyze **the mindset of those around us.** As previously discussed, the mindsets that will be of interest include **levels of dominance, relationships with their environment, perceived need for protection, and familiarity with their surroundings.** Mindset is the physical manifestation of what an individual feels internally about their current situation.

- Finally, we observe **the behaviors of individuals.** While behavior analysis is critical, it is **not** the **first** step in an awareness plan. **Behavioral observations should be focused on individuals who stand out within their environment.** This includes those whose **attention is directed toward something questionable** and those who display **a mindset that suggests ulterior motives inconsistent with their surroundings.**

Understanding behaviors is not a difficult skill to develop, and there are countless books, websites, and articles on the topic. As you have read through this book, many examples likely seemed familiar. **This is because body language is universal—your mind already understands it.** The goal of this book is to provide **words** for the thoughts and feelings you have already experienced while observing behaviors. **The truth about body language is that you didn't need this book to learn about behaviors—you needed words for what you already knew.**

Now that you have the words, **you need a plan** to apply your new skills. Trying to absorb an entire book's worth of knowledge while watching people in a coffee shop can be overwhelming. It is best to **follow a structured plan.**

M.A.C.E.

Mindset – Attention – Comfort – Environment

M.A.C.E. is a simple, effective framework that helps refine **behavioral awareness** into a practical system. When observing those around us, **a structured approach** makes the process more efficient. These are the four key elements to assess in any environment:

Mindset:

- Does this person display a **dedicated or focused** mindset?

- Is their **posture strong and confident?**
- Is their mindset **dominant or submissive?**

Attention:

- Is their focus directed **toward one item or direction, or multiple?**
- Can you **account for and articulate** the reason for their focus?

Comfort:

- Does their body language indicate they are **open or closed?**
- Do they **feel the need for protection** from something?
- How do they feel about their **proximity to others?**

Environment:

- Do they look **comfortable or uncomfortable** in their surroundings?
- Are they **familiar with the environment, or do they appear foreign** to it?
- Do their behaviors **match the expected behaviors for this environment?**
- If not, **can you justify the inconsistency?**

Mastering this subject requires **disciplining yourself to make these observations automatically** as part of your daily life. Without this effort, the knowledge gained from this book remains theoretical.

Attention is a choice. However, being attentive **does not** mean constantly watching every person, movement, or place. **It means having a plan for observing your surroundings.** This plan should be **easy to implement, versatile enough to become a habit, and ultimately a natural part of your daily life.**

Use the table below as a study aid. Position yourself in a public setting and begin profiling your surroundings. In the beginning, **take it slow—there is no need to feel overwhelmed.** Developing situational awareness should feel **natural, not forced.**

M.A.C.E Mindset – Attention – Comfort – Environment

Mindset	Attention	Comfort	Environment
Responsive	Pointing: Upper Zones	Open/Closed	Orderly
Contemplative	Pointing: Lower Zones	Forward/Back	Disorderly
Defensive	Interest	Self-Conscience	Organized
Aggressive	Disinterest	Fearful	Disorganized
Protective	Escape/Evasion	Confident	Purpose
Submissive	Focused	Behavior Speed	Baseline
Dominant	Unfocused	Rigidness	Expected Behaviors
Expectant	Distracted	Proximity +/-	Flagged Behaviors
Mission/Operator		Anxiety	

Exercises

5 Weeks to Behavioral Awareness

Week #1: Comfort and Attention

Exercise 1:

Observe two subjects engaged in a social interaction for approximately 30 seconds and report your findings:

- Classify each individual as **open** or **closed**.
- Identify where they are pointing (using the eight-zone system).
- Assess the comfort level between the subjects.

Exercise 2:

Engage a stranger in a social interaction for 30 seconds and report your findings:

- Was their body language open or closed prior to your arrival?
- Did it change during the interaction? If so, how?
- Describe how and where the subject pointed during the interaction.
- Assess the comfort level of the subject during your interaction.

Week 2: Communication Mindset

Instructions: This exercise will utilize the **Basic Social Baseline Table**. Fill in the traits associated with the following mindsets:

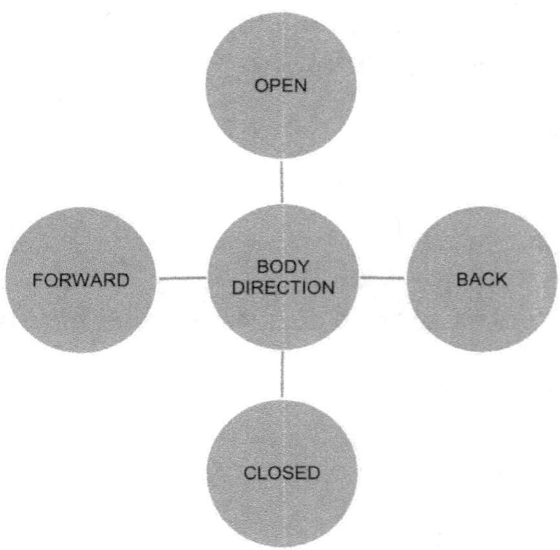

- **Aggressive**
- **Defensive**
- **Contemplative**
- **Responsive**

Locate and describe a person who exhibits each of these mindsets. Provide details about their social interactions.

Week 3: Mindset Awareness

Instructions: Choose a public area where you have a clear view of its inhabitants.

Exercise 1: Identify individuals nearby who are exhibiting the following mindsets:

- **Dominant**
- **Submissive**
- **Comfortable**
- **Uncomfortable**

Exercise 2: Identify individuals who are exhibiting the following mindsets:

- **Interested**
- **Disinterested**
- **Protective**
- **Unprotected**

Exercise 3: Identify individuals who are exhibiting the following mindsets regarding their surroundings:

- **Familiar**
- **Unfamiliar**

Make detailed notes of the behaviors that contribute to these mindsets.

Week 4: Mindset Awareness

Instructions: Choose a public area where you can observe people.

Exercise 1: Identify individuals who are exhibiting the following mindsets:

- **Aggression**
- **Weakness**
- **Submission**
- **Strength**

Analyze their behavior using the following body language indicators:

- **Verbal cues**
- **Physical movements**
- **Eye contact**
- **Posture**

Make detailed notes of the individual behaviors that correspond to each mindset.

Week 5: Communication Mindset

Instructions: This exercise will utilize the **Environmental Baseline Table**.

Each day, visit a different location and identify the following:

- **Classify the environment** based on the table (e.g., *Orderly/Organized*).
- **Identify expected behaviors** in that environment.
- **Note any flagged behaviors** that stand out.

Record observations about the environmental factors that contribute to both expected and flagged behaviors.

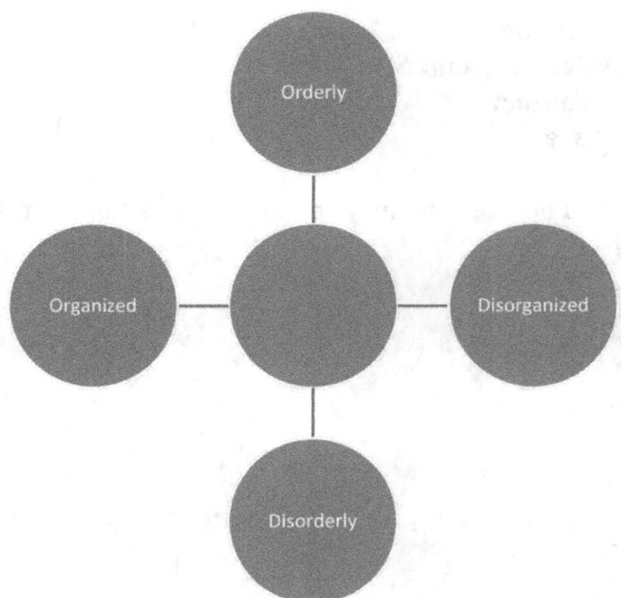

Visit a location each day and identify the following

- Label the environment according to the table above

Example: Orderly/Organized

- Identify expected behaviors
- Establish flagged behaviors

Make notes of the individual environmental factors that establish expected and flagged behaviors

Appendix

Behaviors - Body Language - Gestures

The Head

Head Tilt:

The head tilt is a sign of thinking and comprehension. When someone tilts their head while you are talking, it means they are paying attention. When you ask them a question, they are thinking of the best answer. If the head tilt is combined with squinted eyes, this could indicate confusion or misunderstanding.

Head Jerk:

If someone jerks their head away from you or another person during a conversation, it may symbolize creating a barrier or distancing themselves from what was said. It can also indicate shock, fear, or offense in response to the situation or comment.

Head Nodding:

The head nod symbolizes agreement, understanding, and encouragement for communication. People who nod excessively may be "pleasers" who are incapable of disagreement and may also be insecure or fear rejection. There is safety in agreement.

Head Cradling:

This gesture signals high stress, discomfort, or despair. Cradling the head provides comfort and a feeling of security during hardship or emotional distress.

The Head Bow:

Bowing the head during communication conveys uncertainty, unhappiness, submission, or low self-esteem. Be aware of possible religious or social obligations present. When someone lowers their head or assumes a submissive gesture after speaking, they may be unsure if what they said was correct or questioning whether an attempted deception was believable.

The Chin:

If someone thrusts their chin out or forward, it denotes anger, defiance, and hostility. If someone retracts their chin, they feel threatened or fearful. Stroking the chin is usually a sign of concentration or decision-making. Covering the chin typically signals distrust or suspicion.

The Eyes

Gazing:

Frequent gazing at someone denotes connection and interest. It is a positive, inviting gesture that signals openness to communication. *(Not to be confused with constant staring or glaring.)*

Eyes Open Wide:

This gesture, distinct from the eyebrow flash, denotes interest or enjoyment in what they are seeing. In some cases, it may also indicate shock or amazement.

Avoiding Gaze:

Avoiding eye contact can indicate lying, guilt, or discomfort with the subject being discussed. However, if someone looks away after prolonged eye contact, it may simply mean they are "taking a break" or distancing themselves from the topic.

Eyebrow Flash:

This is when someone opens their eyes wide and raises their eyebrows. It conveys a friendly "hello" and is designed to disarm others from a distance. It also signals, "talk to me," "I'll talk to you," or "help me." This is a non-threatening, non-dominant submissive cue.

Lowering the Eyebrows:

This gesture portrays seriousness. It can indicate a threatening mindset or distrust of a situation. If combined with a head tilt, it suggests disbelief.

Looking Up:

Lowering one's head while looking up at someone can express skepticism or disbelief. This gesture can be perceived as either a threatening look or an expression of doubt.

Blinking:

- **Prolonged blinking (slow-motion blinking):** Indicates boredom, disinterest, or even sleepiness. If accompanied by a raised eyebrow, it suggests waning attention. To regain engagement, change the conversation or ask a question.
- **Excessive blinking:** Can indicate romantic interest or signs of stress, depending on the situation. It may also be a cue associated with heightened mental activity.

Rolling the Eyes:

This gesture denotes disagreement, boredom, or exasperation. If very pronounced, it signals strong frustration. If someone frequently rolls their eyes, they may soon lose interest in the conversation.

Pupil Size:

Pupils dilate (widen) to take in more light, which assists vision. Similarly, they widen when someone is experiencing interest, excitement, intense thought, sexual attraction, or pain. Conversely, pupils constrict when someone feels an aversion or dislike. If constriction is accompanied by disgust, the viewer likely finds something unpleasant.

The Face

Touching:

Excessive touching of the face, especially the nose, often indicates deception or an attempt to hide something.

Ears:

Tugging on the ears signifies indecisiveness or confusion. It can also indicate an aversion to what is being said.

Nose:

Pinching the bridge of the nose is usually a sign of high stress or frustration.

Pursed Lips:

Pursed lips suggest heightened anxiety, anger, or fear. They may also indicate a perceived threat.

Off-Centered Lips:

This expression denotes boredom or a mocking mindset. It can also be an exaggerated sign of decision-making.

Exhaled Lips:

Exhaling with puffed lips suggests exhaustion or boredom. If combined with eye-rolling, it may signal mockery.

Sneer:

A sneer conveys strong feelings of contempt, anger, or negative emotions.

Sideways Glance:

Looking left or right without moving the head can indicate hostility in certain contexts when paired with other negative cues. However, it may also show curiosity or an attempt to observe someone discreetly.

The Arms

Arms Crossed:

This gesture suggests the person feels the need for protection, is uncomfortable, or is closed off to suggestions. While crossed arms may not always indicate defensiveness, they can be a more telling indicator if combined with other cues, such as clenched fists or tension in the shoulders.

Arms Crossed with Clenched Fists:

This posture indicates hostility, often bordering on aggression.

Arms Open:

An open-arm posture suggests confidence, openness to suggestion, and relaxation.

Excited Arms and Hands:

When someone's hands and arms seem overly animated during conversation, it denotes enthusiasm or excitement. However, excessive gestures may indicate a need for attention. Passionate gestures should not be confused with exaggerated "over-the-top" movements.

Ready Arms:

A stance with slightly bent arms signals a "take charge" attitude and a sense of control.

Arm Swings:

Restless, repetitive arm movements may indicate an unconscious desire to leave or escape the situation.

Arms Crossed with Thumbs Exposed:

Crossed arms with visible thumbs suggest confidence or a belief in one's superiority.

Stiff Arm:

A stiffly extended arm is a defensive gesture, often used to establish personal space or signal "stop."

The Hands

Seen Palms:

Visible palms indicate truthfulness, credibility, and openness.

Unseen Palms:

Hidden or closed palms suggest a closed-off attitude, possible deception, or discomfort.

Pointing:

Pointing is an assertive, sometimes intimidating gesture. It conveys authority and confidence but can also appear aggressive.

Hands on Head:

Placing hands behind the head suggests frustration or dislike of a topic.

Thumbs on a Gesture:

Using the thumbs in gestures conveys confidence, superiority, or even arrogance. If used while pointing, it can signal ridicule or disrespect.

Single Hand in Pants Pocket:

Placing one hand in a pocket may appear casual, but it often indicates discomfort or unease in the present situation.

The Legs and Feet

Open Legs:

An open-leg posture suggests comfort and openness to suggestion. However, gender differences should be considered in leg positioning.

Crossing Legs:

Crossing the legs at the ankles signals ease. However, locking the feet or ankles suggests hesitation or anxiety.

Bouncing Feet:

Jiggling, bouncing, or tapping the feet usually signals boredom or impatience, rather than irritation.

Pointing Feet:

Feet often point toward what a person is interested in. If someone's feet are turned toward a door, they may want to leave. If trying to influence someone, positioning your feet toward them can signal engagement and focus.

The Body

Security Blanket:

People often draw objects such as purses, jackets, or coffee cups closer to their bodies for comfort in uncomfortable situations. This gesture resembles a child clutching a teddy bear for security.

"Shield" Objects:

Using objects (e.g., jewelry, watches, phones, drinks) as a barrier—especially if placed across the body—suggests a subconscious need for protection. This behavior is often seen in situations where the person perceives a threat, even if the threat is only psychological.

References

Chappell, J. T. (2017, June 14). NPR.org . Retrieved from National Public Radio : https://www.npr.org/sections/thetwo-way/2017/06/14/532951612/what-witnesses-saw-when-gunfire-struck-a-congressional-baseball-practice

Christopher Chabris, D. S. (2010). The invisible Gorilla. Retrieved from The invisible Gorilla : http://www.theinvisiblegorilla.com/videos.html

Daniel J. Simpson, D. T. (2003). What Makes Change Blindness Interesting? Psychology of Learning and Motivation, 295-322.

Ekman, P. (1975). Unmasking the Face. Prentice Hall.

Ekman, P. (1993). Facial Expressions of Emotion (Vol. 48. American Psychologist.

Ekman, P. (1994). Strong Evidence for Universals in Facial Expressions: a reply to Russell's mistaken critique. Psychological Bulletin, Vol. 115.

Goffman, E. (1963). Behaviour in Public Places. Free Press.

Lyle E. Bourne, J. R. (2003). STRESS AND COGNITION: A COGNITIVE. University of Colorado.

Philippot, P. C. (2002). Respiratory feedback in the generation of emotion. Cognition and Emotion, 16, 605-627.

Remsberg, C. (2011, December 14). Shot 5 times, a sergeant reflects on lessons learned. Retrieved from Police One: https://www.policeone.com/officer-shootings/articles/4832978-Shot-5-times-a-sergeant-reflects-on-lessons-learned/

Riley, P. V. (2014). Left Of Bang. Black Irish Entertainment LLC.